KAREN COMMINGS

The Dog Lover's Survival Guide:

Helpful Hints for Solving Your Most Pesky Pet Problems

BARRON'S

ACKNOWLEDGMENTS

I would like to express my sincere thanks to these people, who provided me with information, tips, and suggestions: Donna Allen, Fenda Alp (American Pet Products Manufacturers Association), Allan Arthur, Carol Banks, Jackie Burgen, Jane Buxton and Morgan the guide dog, Barb Eichorn, Judy Heim, Dana R. Miller, Mary Osterberg, Catherine S. Perel, Bonnie Rayho, Erica Marie Stark, Eileen A. Stone, and Steve Wayland (program director, PAWS/LA).

● ● ●

All inquiries should be addressed to:
Barron's Educational Series, Inc.
250 Wireless Boulevard
Hauppauge, NY 11788
http://www.barronseduc.com

International Standard Book No. 0-7641-1575-8
Library of Congress Catalog Card No. 00-059889

Library of Congress Cataloging-in-Publication Data
Commings, Karen.
    The dog lover's survival guide: helpful hints for solving your most
    pesky pet problems / Karen Commings.
        p. cm.
    ISBN 0-7641-1575-8
    1. Dogs. I. Title.
SF427.C66 2001
636.7'088'7—dc21   00-059889

Printed in the United States of America
9 8 7 6 5 4 3 2 1

Contents

Introduction

Many years ago, I was in an automobile accident. I had no pets at the time, so caring for animals wasn't an issue. Now that I do have pets, I often wonder how I would care for them if an accident left me wheelchair-bound as it did for the three months following my accident. When I temporarily lost vision in my left eye about ten years ago, I spent much of the two weeks it took to regain my sight thinking about how I would care for my pets if I lost my sight permanently. How would I know if one of them was sick? How would I be able to tell them apart? How would I tell what flavor of food I was feeding them?

Although I'm in good health now, I began to seek answers to some of these questions in the event that my health ever fails. What if a physical disability kept me from caring for my pets as I do now? How do other people with vision, back, or other physical problems care for their pets? How does a blind person determine where her dog has relieved himself so she can scoop it up? How does someone confined to a wheelchair pull pet food from a kitchen cupboard built for people with full use of their legs? How does someone with back problems fill his dog's food dish or even pick it up from the floor?

These and other questions led me to write the chapter in this book on helping pet owners with physical disabilities in the hope that the tips would help them keep their pets when the disability might cause them to think about finding the pet another home.

Even if you do not suffer from a physical difficulty, the tips in this book will help you spend more time with your dog and less time performing some of the more mundane tasks involved in pet care. Isn't throwing a Frisbee for your dog more fun than vacuuming his hair from the floor or unclogging a drain after you give him a bath? If you are like me, you would rather spend time enjoying your pets than cleaning up after them. *The Dog Lover's Survival Guide* will help you keep cleanup time to a minimum and help you solve some of those other pesky pet problems as well—from behavior and safety issues to finding the best way for you and Rover to travel. Enjoy the time and effort you save by spending it with your dog.

Cleaning Tips

Unlike the thrill of observing your dog's enthusiasm as he anticipates a good game of fetch, the boredom of cleaning up after him can be both tiresome and trying. Housebreaking a puppy goes a long way in reducing the amount of time you will have to spend cleaning up your dog's accidents. For additional help cutting down the cleanup time, try some of the ideas in this chapter.

Cleanliness is next to...

Perhaps Fido had a potty accident while waiting for you to come home from the office after working late. He tried to hold it but just couldn't manage. Or maybe Buster occasionally upchucks his dinner when he eats too fast. Following are some ways to keep periodic accidents from becoming permanent memories.

• Premix in spray bottles appropriate cleaning products, such as vinegar and water or detergent and water, so the products are handy when you need them. Label the spray bottles with their contents and store them in a convenient location. Often, just the strength of the spray on the spot where Fido accidentally left you a present helps lift up the residue and prevent stains from forming.

• Upholstered furniture comes in all styles and fabrics; some are easy to clean and some are more difficult. To help us with our cleaning chores, manufacturers have marked their furniture with a cleaning code or set of instructions to let the consumer know what type of cleaning is recommended for that fabric.

The codes are usually on the furniture platforms under the cushions. A "W," for example, means that the product should be cleaned only with water, while the letter "S" means the furniture should be cleaned only with solvents. Before using any cleaning product on your upholstered furniture, check the manufacturer's instructions and test-clean a spot in an inconspicuous place.

• Treat your carpet and upholstered furniture with a stain-resistant product such as Scotchgard.

HOW-TO: Remove Urine from Carpet

*Most carpet manufacturers print care instructions for the carpet they produce. If you have older carpeting or don't know the name of the manufacturer, follow these easy steps to remove urine when your pet has an accident. **A word of caution: Never use ammonia on a urine spot. Urine is ammonia-based and will entice your dog to return to the spot to relieve himself.***

If you can smell telltale urine in your carpet but can't find it, use a black light to pinpoint the spots to make cleaning the carpet easier.

1. *Blot up the urine as quickly as possible with a dry cloth or paper towel.*
2. *Apply a small amount of diluted detergent solution consisting of 1/4 teaspoon of mild liquid dish-washing detergent and one quart of water, or use a solution of 1/4 cup of vinegar and one quart of water.*
3. *Press the solution into the urine spot and continue to blot up the excess. Do not rub the urine into the carpet.*
4. *Rinse the spot with clear water or an odor neutralizer and blot dry.*
5. *Place paper towels or clean, dry cloths over the area and weight them down. Change the paper towels or cloths as soon as they have become saturated with liquid and apply dry ones. Continue this process until the carpet is dry.*
6. *After the spot has dried, brush up the piling and vacuum the area. Be sure the spot is completely dry before walking on it.*

Germ Warfare

In the total scheme of things, we stand to catch more harmful germs from other people or even the food we eat than we do from animals, but eliminating bacteria from surfaces on which our dogs walk or from our hands can help make our homes and us more sanitary. Here are some weapons for your war against germs.

• If you're on a walk with your dog, take along an individually packaged antibacterial wipe to clean and sanitize your hands after picking up your dog's wastes. Antibacterial wipes are available in supermarkets and grocery stores.

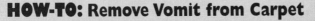

HOW-TO: Remove Vomit from Carpet

Dogs may vomit because they have eaten too fast, especially if they must compete with other pets for food, they are overheated, or they are stressed. If your dog vomits more than three times in a six-hour period, have him examined by a veterinarian. If you are faced with removing vomit from carpet, the best solution is to let the vomit dry, then vacuum it up. If you don't have that option, follow the steps below. Food with added dyes can discolor fabric or carpet if your pet vomits his dinner, so it's best to clean up the deposit as quickly as possible.

1. *Use a spoon or fork to remove solid or dried materials from the vomit.*
2. *If the stain is large, work from the outside to the center to prevent it from spreading. Blot up any liquid with a paper towel or cloth.*
3. *Apply a solution of one teaspoon of detergent or one cup of vinegar to one quart of water to the area, then dampen the area with a cloth. If you use a brush, lightly brush the area in one direction so you don't damage the carpet fibers.*
4. *If necessary, put on some rubber gloves and work the detergent solution into the carpet.*
5. *Wet the carpet with clear water to rinse.*
6. *Place clean paper towels or clean cloths on the area and weight them down. Change the paper towels or cloths when they have absorbed liquid.*
7. *After the spot has dried, brush up the piling and vacuum the area. Be sure the spot is completely dry before walking on it.*

• Use common household bleach to wipe down surfaces or clean floors to eliminate harmful bacteria. Rinse well and don't allow your dog to walk on the surface while it's wet. If the bleach gets on your dog's paws, he might ingest it when he licks his feet. *Caution: Pretest a surface before cleaning with bleach to avoid color changes.*

• Or, use an antibacterial cleaner with an odor neutralizer to remove bacteria and leave your house clean smelling.

• After scooping the doggie-doo, use an antibacterial soap to wash your hands.

• Wash dog food dishes with detergent on a daily basis to prevent bacterial growth. If your dog's food and water bowls are dishwasher safe, place them in the dishwasher where the high temperatures will kill bacteria.

Hair and There

Do you arrive at the office looking like you rolled over with your dog? Do your dinner guests politely pick dog hair from their food before eating it? Nothing says "I have a dog" more than hair clinging to our clothing, hair wafting through the air in our homes, or hair burrowing into the butter. Frequent vacuuming is one of the best ways to cut down on hair buildup, but if you don't always have time to drag out the vacuum cleaner, try some of these quick and dirty suggestions for cleaning up the piles of pet hair.

• To sweep up loose dog hair from hardwood or vinyl floors, use a dampened mop.

• Wall-to-wall carpeting holds down the hair more than hardwood or vinyl floors, so adding a carpet to a room may help keep dog hair from wafting through your house.

• To pick up loose dog hair that is attached to upholstered furniture, wear a dampened rubber glove or use a damp sponge.

- Use a sticky roller to lift dog hair from fabrics and upholstery. Washable sticky rollers enable you to recycle instead of dispose of the product.

- Purchase a washable FURniture Magnet Pet Hair Remover to help you wipe off the dog hair from clothing, furniture, or pillows. Place it under your furniture cushions for easy access.

- To pick up dog hair from your carpet, use a window squeegee.

- Choose furniture made from smooth fabrics such as leather, faux leather, or other fabric to which loose hair won't stick as readily.

- Place a washable towel or blanket over your dog's favorite sleeping spot to keep hair from clinging to cushions.

- Use washable window coverings if your dog likes to watch the world go by from the floor in front of a picture window or patio doors.

- Draperies made of smooth fabrics won't attract as much hair as heavy textured ones, so if you're in the market for some new window furnishings, purchase ones that are less likely to become filled with your dog's hair.

- Keep a lint brush near your favorite easy chair. Then, after your dog sits on your lap, you can roll off the hair before you get up.

- Use a feather duster or device to clean between slats of mini-blinds to remove deposited hair.

- Change the furnace and air conditioner filters more often during shedding season to prevent blockage.

Hair on clothes

- Remove dog hair from your clothing with a dampened rubber glove, sticky roller, or masking tape, or blow it off with a blow-dryer.

• Keep a roll of masking tape or a sticky roller in your car to remove dog hair after you leave the house. Keep some in your office drawer at work to do the same.

Hair on bedding

• Run your bedding through the air-dry or fluff cycle of your dryer to remove hair before putting it in the washing machine.

• If some dog hair remains at the bottom of the washing machine after you've done your laundry, remove the hair by running the washer through one rinse cycle.

Hair in drains

• If your dog's hair accompanies you into the shower and clogs the drain, or your drains run slowly after giving your dog a bath, keep a plunger handy. Hand plungers come in many sizes for different-sized drains. Some have short handles for de-clogging a sink, and others have longer handles to reach the drains in a tub or shower. Plunge after each use to keep the dog hair from severely clogging your drains.

• Purchase a mechanical plunger for those hairy pipes. All types of plungers are available in hardware stores and builders' outlets.

• Place steel wool in your drain to catch hair.

Managing the Pet Poop

With pets, poop piles are as inevitable as death and taxes. Even though we don't like to think about it, waste management goes with the pet ownership territory. Picking up after our dogs when we walk them is a good way to enhance our relationships with neighbors, especially if Fido has chosen their front yards in which to make a deposit. If piles of pet poop get you down, try some of these suggestions to keep from being overwhelmed by your dog's wastes.

• Feeding a highly digestible, high-quality food will reduce the volume of stools your dog passes.

• A long-handled scoop and rake will make the poop-scooping chore go faster.

• If the poop is piling up faster than you can get rid of it, investigate any local services that perform poop scooping. Occasionally, pet-sitters also will do poop scooping as a sideline to their pet-sitting services. Check the Yellow Pages under Pets or Pet-sitters, or inquire about such services at a local pet store.

• Purchase cardboard doggie doo pickup pouches at your local pet store. Their unique shape enables you to pick up your dog's waste and fold the container closed for disposal.

• If your dog deposits small amounts of stools on his walk, use zip-closure plastic food bags to pick up the waste.

• If your dog has trouble holding it if you are working late or when you can't get home at lunchtime to walk him, investigate using a dog-walking service. Check the Yellow Pages under Pets or Pet-sitters.

• If your dog eliminates before you have a chance to come home and take him for a walk, try placing some newspaper covered with an absorbent doggie pad near his favorite potty place to prevent soiling your carpet or floor. Absorbent pet potty pads or training pads are available in pet stores.

• Check out your local pet store or a pet supplies catalog for complete doggie waste removal systems that keep your backyard from smelling like a doggie dump.

The Nose Knows

No matter how often our dogs wash themselves or we wash them, sometimes just having a dog in the house can leave a telltale smell. Long after the stain is lifted, doggie odors can linger. Follow some of these suggestions to keep from being entrenched in stench.

• Bathing your dog regularly will help cut down doggie odors. If it's too cold to bathe him, use a dry shampoo or massage some baking soda into your dog's coat and brush it out to remove odors.

• Purchase an electronic air-cleaning system designed to remove doggie odors from the air.

• Make your own carpet freshener by combining one box of baking soda with one tablespoon of orris root (available in herb stores) that has been saturated in your favorite scented oil. Place the mixture in a glass jar and cover with a metal lid in which you've punched holes. Let it sit for a few days so that the baking soda picks up the oil scent then sprinkle it onto the carpet before vacuuming. The jar lid will prevent the orris root from spilling out, so you can reuse it by just adding more baking soda. Sprinkle the mixture onto the carpet, let sit for 15 or 20 minutes, then vacuum up.

• Use a window fan set on exhaust to make odor elimination a breeze.

• Odors and stains from feces or urine are protein-based and require an odor neutralizer containing bacterial enzymes to completely eliminate them. Purchase enzyme products at discount department stores, health stores, or pet stores. If you attend a dog show, you may find vendors who sell odor neutralizers intended to eliminate pet odors. Odor neutralizers may be added to the laundry to remove odors from bedding and leave it smelling clean.

Post-meal Cleanup

Unless you are cooking your dog's meals instead of serving them from a bag, box, or can, after-meal cleanup should not be complicated. But let's face it, some dogs, like some people, are just sloppy eaters. Instead of trying to improve your dog's mealtime manners, try some of these suggestions.

• To make cleaning your dog's food bowls easier, coat them with vegetable cooking spray to keep food from sticking on the bottom.

• An alternative to using cooking spray on your dog's bowls is to purchase nonstick bowls for him. Nonstick bowls are available in kitchen stores or housewares departments.

• To keep food from flying onto the floor around your dog's food dish, place the dish on a tray instead of a place mat.

• Plastic salad bar containers with lid and bottom still connected can become food and water dishes or a tray on which to place your dog's regular bowl to keep food and water from spilling.

• If you are caring for a litter of puppies that have been weaned, competition for food may become intense. Instead of giving each one a separate dish, try feeding them from a muffin tin to keep cleanup chores to a minimum.

Smudges and Streaks

Does your dog enjoy watching the world go by from the glass patio doors? If so, you may have smudges and streaks from his pressing his nose against the glass to get a better view. Keeping your dog away from doors deprives him of one of the supreme pleasures of an indoor pet, but if you want to keep up with elimination of smudges and streaks, follow some of these suggestions.

- Compromise with your dog and designate one or two locations as lookout spots. Place objects or plants in the other locations so that your dog cannot access those places.

- In a spray bottle, mix one part vinegar to three parts water as a glass cleaner and keep it handy. Clean with a lint-free cloth or squeegee dry.

- To prevent your dog from smudging glass in doors, choose gathered curtains that are held down by a curtain rod at the top and bottom so that he can't get his nose to the glass.

Cost-Saving Tips

Americans spend more than 23 billion dollars annually on pet food, products, services, and veterinary care. There probably are times when you feel like you're financing the pet industry yourself.

Although you won't want to skimp on your dog's health or nutritional needs, there are some ways to save money on his care. Whether you have one dog or a dozen, the following techniques will help your doggie care dollars stretch a little further.

General Cost-Saving Hints

• One of the nice features of dog shows—besides seeing so many beautiful animals—is the plethora of vendors who set up shop to sell their wares to those who enter and attend the show. The products are often cheaper than products you find in a pet store, so relax and enjoy the show and stock up on pet supplies to save some money.

• Clip and use store coupons on food and dog items. If you have more coupons than you can use, place extras in the pet aisles of your grocery store or donate them to a local shelter or animal organization.

• Watch ads in your local newspapers for sales at local pet stores and pet warehouses. You may find buy-one-and-get-one free promotions or even obtain premium food and products at minimal costs.

• Buy food in larger sizes that are cheaper on an ounce-by-ounce basis.

- Shop at yard sales and flea markets to find items that your dog can use. You may be lucky enough to find inexpensive carriers, beds, bowls, toys, and other items. Be sure to clean them thoroughly before use!

- Take advantage of manufacturers' promotional sales. These often come with added pet products for minimal costs. Although some promotions require you to send away for the products, the cost of postage is less than the cost of the product if you had to buy it.

Bedding Down

Go into any pet store or shop in any pet supply catalog, and you'll find doggie beds in a myriad of styles to match any decor. Although lovely, dog beds can be pretty pricey, leaving us to wonder why we would want to spend so much money on something our dogs use with their eyes closed. The cheapest way to provide your dog with a bed is to let him share yours, but if you'd like him to have his own sleeping quarters at a lower cost than those you find at retail prices, here are some ideas.

- Shop at flea markets for old wooden shipping crates. Line them with blankets for a comfy sleeping spot.

- Purchase dog beds that have washable covers to prevent replacing the beds as often.

- At flea markets and yard sales, buy old quilts or blankets for your dog's bedding. Again, wash them thoroughly before use.

- Save your old towels and blankets for your dog to sleep on.

• Fill an old pillowcase with a soft piece of foam rubber. Sew the end shut. You will have a comfortable, washable dog bed, and your dog will appreciate having a bed made from something that is yours.

Cleaning Up

Cleaning generally requires more effort than expense, but some commercial cleaning products can cost an arm and a leg. If you'd like to reduce the expense of cleaning up after your dog, try some of these low-cost alternatives.

• Baking soda makes an excellent, cheap alternative for cleaning marks from the corners of your walls. It also can be used as a dry shampoo for your dog.

HOW-TO: Make a T-shirt Pet Bed

A bed made from one of your old T-shirts will be especially appealing to your small dog, or, if you have an old sleep shirt, use this technique to make a bed for your large dog. Making your pet a T-shirt bed will be emotionally rewarding and save you money at the same time. The T-shirt bed can be machine-washed and dried when it becomes dirty. All you need are one of your old T-shirts, some cotton batting or fiberfill, and thread.

1. *Sew the armholes and neck hole of the shirt closed.*
2. *Fill the top half of the shirt with whatever washable stuffing you choose.*
3. *Sew a seam across the midsection of the shirt just below the arms to trap the stuffing in the top half.*
4. *Sew another seam from the center of the midsection seam to the bottom of the shirt, creating two sections in the lower half of the T-shirt.*
5. *Stuff both sections, then sew the bottom shut.*
6. *Fold over the sleeves and hand-stitch them to the underside of the bed.*

You have created a dog bed with three pillowed sections. Place the bed anywhere your dog likes to sleep—next to a heating vent, on a chair, or under the bed. Your dog will love you for making it.

• As mentioned earlier, if you bathe your dog in a sink or bathtub, dog hair can build up and clog the drain. For less than the price of one container of drain cleaner, you can purchase a hand plunger to remove clogged hair from your pipes.

• Add some white vinegar to the rinse water when you wash your dog's bedding to remove odors or rinse your dog with one part vinegar to four parts water after a bath.

Food and Water Bowls

Dogs don't care what their food and water bowls look like—only what's in them. Dog food bowls are designed for the owner rather than the dog. Your dog will love you just as much if you provide his nourishment in an old pie plate as he will if you offer it in a specially made doggie bowl. Instead of spending money on something that won't make a difference in your dog's well-being, try one of these low-cost solutions to pet platters.

• If your dog eats dry and canned food, serve it on a divided plate such as those used for picnics instead of providing two bowls.

• Place your dog's food bowls on an old rubber dish drainer to prevent spills and keep bits and pieces of food from falling onto the floor.

• Another idea for a pet place mat is to use the shallow cardboard cartons in which cases of dog food are sold. For extra protection of your floors, leave the plastic covering on the cardboard case before placing your dog's food and water bowls in it.

• If your dog leaves some of his canned food in his bowl to snack on later, cover the dish with a lightweight plastic container, such as a cottage cheese container, to keep the food from drying out. Your dog should be able to knock the lid off to get to the food when he is hungry. If he has trouble with the concept, show him how to remove the cover until he learns the technique for himself.

• Instead of bowls, use heavy glass ashtrays available at dollar stores. The weight keeps them from sliding around the floor.

• Visit flea markets and yard sales to find inexpensive bowls to use for your dog's food.

Health Care Solutions

Your dog deserves the best veterinary care to help him live a long and happy life. Providing your dog with annual checkups, vaccinations, and medical care when he needs it is one way to ensure that the two of you spend many years together. There are some ways, however, to reduce the costs of basic health care.

• Spaying or neutering your dog prevents the births and deaths of unwanted puppies. It also helps prevent certain types of cancer and inappropriate behaviors associated with the reproductive cycle. Many geographic locations have low-cost spay and neuter organizations. If you adopted your dog from a shelter, he or she might have received the surgery before you adopted him or her. If you adopted a pedigreed dog from a breeder, the breeder may have spayed or neutered the animal prior to sale. If your pet has not been sexually altered, contact a local shelter, animal organization, or veterinarian to determine if low-cost spaying and neutering are available. If you cannot find a local group, contact SPAY USA, a network of volunteers and veterinarians working together to popularize and facilitate spay/neuter services through a nationwide toll-free referral service. SPAY USA is operated by the North Shore Animal League, Long Island, New York.

• Some shelters operate veterinary clinics to serve the needs of the animals that are surrendered to them. In some cases, the shelter-run clinics are open to the public and may offer veterinary services at a lower cost than veterinarians in private practice. Contact the shelters in your area to see if they offer veterinary services.

• States in which rabies is more prevalent may require that you obtain an annual rabies shot for your dog. Local shelters and animal organizations may offer rabies shots administered by their own veterinarians at a lower cost than your veterinarian might. Contact the shelters in your area to determine if they have a low-cost rabies vaccination program.

• If you have more than one dog, ask your veterinarian if he or she offers multi-pet discounts.

• Veterinary health insurance is available to cover your dog's medical needs. Insurance varies in cost and what it will cover. Discuss with your veterinarian insurance options that may help you save money on your dog's health care.

• If you are planning to adopt two dogs at the same time from a shelter, ask if the shelter offers a discount on the second dog. Many shelters will reduce the cost for adoption when a prospective pet parent wants to adopt more than one.

Pet Playthings

When it comes to play, *dogs just wanna have fun.* Your dog will enjoy the workout as much or more than the toy when you involve him in a favorite game. Commercially available toys are wonderful, but they can be costly. To provide your dog with inexpensive playthings, try some of these low-cost or no-cost alternatives.

• Give your dog those old socks that are full of holes or ones that have lost their mates. Tie them in a knot and give them to your dog to chew or toss. ***Caution: Be sure to put your good socks away so that your dog doesn't think that all socks are potential playthings.***

• Instead of buying toys for your dog to retrieve, find some sturdy sticks to fling for him.

- Throw an old tennis ball for your dog to chase and get some exercise.

- Visit flea markets and yard sales to find children's old stuffed toys that can be used as dog toys. Very often, these toys have been cleaned and are ready for the next owner. Dogs will enjoy biting and tossing them. *Caution: Be sure to remove any small parts, such as beaded eyes, from the toys so that your dog doesn't accidentally swallow them.*

- Let your dog chase the light from a flashlight as you move it around the floor or up the walls.

Pet Poop

Wouldn't you rather spend your money on what goes into your dog's mouth than cleaning up what comes out the other end? Here are some low-cost alternative ways to avoid wasting money on your dog's wastes.

- Save the plastic bags that come with the daily newspaper to use as poop scoopers. Insert your hand into the bag and pick up the pile. Turn the bag inside out and tie it up for disposal.

- Save your produce bags from the grocery store to use for doggie-doo pickup.

Resources

SPAY/USA, 1-800-248-SPAY

You will receive information about the nearest low-cost program and will be sent a certificate as proof you have gone through the SPAY/USA network.

NORTH SHORE ANIMAL LEAGUE
Davis Avenue
Port Washington, NY 11050
516-883-4558

Safety Tips

If your dog has a close call with an automobile, he will have no air bag handy to protect him. If your mild-mannered dog comes into contact with a wild-mannered animal, he may get more than the wind knocked out of him. Even if your dog has been vaccinated against contagious diseases, contracting one for which there is no defense may be a bitter pill to swallow. While our homes are not entirely free of potential hazards, keeping dogs leashed when outside increases their safety and the safety of our neighbors. We can further eliminate potential hazards by making our homes safer places in which our dogs can live.

Disaster Preparedness

At various times of the year, Mother Nature casts her wrath and fury upon us in the form of tornadoes, hurricanes, floods, fires, earthquakes, snowstorms, and even volcanos. Add to the mix manmade emergencies such as chemical spills, explosions, or nuclear power disasters and the potential for wreaking havoc on our lives escalates. In most cases, disaster shelters don't allow pets to wait out the problem with their owners. Often, the family dog is forgotten under such circumstances and left behind to fend for himself until his human family returns. Unfortunately, many dogs don't survive the disaster, or they become stranded, only to be rescued by strangers and never reunited with those they love. Some disasters, such as floods, may last for several weeks, while others, such as snowstorms, may keep us from getting to the grocery store for a few days. Whatever the potential for disaster in your geographic locale, knowing what to do with your dog will help him survive the situation.

• Always take your dog with you or board him at a safe location outside the disaster area. Never leave your dog alone in the home with food and water. Animals can become disoriented and panicked in times of crises. They can upset their water or food bowls. If a door collapses or a window blows in, your dog can easily escape. If a wall or roof caves in, your dog could be crushed and die. In a flood, your dog could drown.

• If you travel frequently and might be away when disaster strikes, having a buddy in the neighborhood who will look after your dog may be his only chance for survival. Being a buddy to a neighbor's dog will help ensure that others' animals are protected in times of distress.

• Put a collar and identification tag on your dog that includes your name and phone number in case he becomes lost or stranded.

• Keep your dog's vaccinations current.

• Know the locations of animal shelters in your area in case you have to visit them if your dog gets lost.

• Contact friends or relatives outside the disaster area for temporary placement of your dog.

• Prepare a list of veterinarians and boarding facilities that might be able to board your dog.

• Contact pet-friendly hotels and motels outside the disaster area that might be able to house you and your dog.

• Keep the results of your research, such as relevant phone numbers and contacts, handy.

• Keep a disaster kit on hand or purchase one. Check your pet stores or mail-order catalogs for ready-made kits or make your own as described on page 22.

Make certain someone else knows about your dog

If someone besides you had to provide care for your dog if an emergency occurred that kept you from doing so, would he or she be able to? Would the person know what, when, and how much your dog eats? Would the person know how often to walk your dog? Would the temporary caregiver know if your dog has any health problems or even who the dog's veterinarian is? One of the ways you can help a relative, friend, or neighbor give your dog temporary care when you can't is to make a doggie folder that tracks your dog's history. The folder should contain descriptions of your dog, up-to-date health information, personality data, and any other useful information that will ensure that he continues to get proper care if you are incapacitated. A folder is also useful to take along if you and your dog are traveling and must obtain emergency veterinary care on the trip.

• Designate a specific individual as your dog's emergency caregiver. Keep the person's name and phone number in your wallet to be notified if something happens to you.

HOW-TO: Make a Disaster Kit for Your Dog

1. *Include at least one month's supply of dog food, a can opener (if necessary), food and water bowls, airtight containers for dry food, some of your dog's favorite treats, a supply of paper towels, antibacterial hand wipes, and several gallons of bottled water. Store the items in covered plastic storage bins that will fit in the interior or trunk of your car. If you have a storm cellar or shelter in your home, store the doggie necessities along with your own.*
2. *Pack a supply of waste disposal bags.*
3. *Pack some familiar bedding, toys, and grooming tools. Your dog will be just as stressed as you.*
4. *Have on hand a backup supply of your dog's medication, such as insulin, as well as the necessary tools to administer the medication, such as needles, syringes, or pill guns.*
5. *Include a pet first aid kit.*
6. *Include your dog's medical records and a current photo.*
7. *Include a carrier or crate for each dog and a strong harness and leash.*

- Place a photo of your dog inside the folder.

- List important information such as the dog's date of birth, breed, sex, color, and markings.

- List your veterinarian's name, address, and phone number.

- Summarize important medical information and keep it current. If you like, place your veterinarian receipts in the folder.

- List the dates of annual checkups and vaccinations.

- List the dates of spay/neuter or other surgery.

- Indicate any medications your dog is taking and how often.

- If your dog is battling a long-term illness, track his symptoms and keep the list in the folder.

- Make a list of important feeding information that includes number and times of daily feedings; types, brands, and quantities of food; any food allergies or problems, such as certain types or brands causing diarrhea; and the location in your house where the food is kept.

- Make a list of any noteworthy behavioral information, such as the dog not liking men or women or children. Describe any problems with other animals or species. List whether your dog has any idiosyncratic bathroom habits, such as not pottying when on a leash.

- Make certain your dog's backup caregiver knows where the folder is kept in the event of an emergency.

Escaping Escapades

Does your dog want to run outside with your children every time they open the door? Are you afraid that your dog will take off after a squirrel or other animal whenever someone leaves or enters your house? Are you afraid he will accidentally escape the safety of his leash when you walk him? If bolting the door is not an option to keep your dog from bolting through it, try some of these suggestions to keep him safely under your control.

• If your dog escapes from his leash when you are out for a walk, lie down and stay still. Your dog will come back to investigate. When he's in reach, grab his collar to regain control. Don't reprimand him for returning to you.

• Keep a squirt gun handy by the door. Lightly spray your dog if he appears to be contemplating a break.

• If you must confine a dog to a room in the home when you have a party that involves visitors coming and going, install a screen door or baby gate to the room to prevent him from feeling isolated.

• Have your dog spayed or neutered. Altered animals are less likely to wander.

• Try clicker-style obedience training. If your dog knows what it means to *stay* or *sit* when you open a door, he is less likely to leave with you. See the Behavior chapter for instructions on how to clicker-train your dog (page 68).

• Install a baby gate on the exterior of the door to prevent your dog from escaping when you leave or enter your home.

• As a preventative measure, provide your dog with some means of identification. Having a collar and identification tags is the quickest way for someone who has found your dog to locate you. When a dog is lost, however, he may lose his collar or tags, so having a secondary form of ID is advisable. Discuss with your veterinarian the options of having your dog tattooed or a microchip implanted. A tattoo involves imprinting a series of numbers and/or letters on your dog. The tattoo ID is then entered into a database and the dog owner is given a tag for the dog's collar that has the toll-free number to help identify him and you. If the tag is lost, anyone finding your dog can contact a shelter or veterinarian to help identify him. Microchips are implanted by a veterinarian under the dog's skin. Like the tattoo, the chip's code is entered into a national database. To identify a lost animal with an implanted microchip, veterinarians or shelters use a special scanner.

HOW-TO: Find a Lost Pet

Before you begin combing the neighborhood looking for your dog, make sure he is not trapped or hiding somewhere in your home. A small dog may be napping somewhere sight unseen. Bring along a smelly treat or favorite noise-making toy to get a hiding dog's attention. Once you have determined that your dog is missing, follow these steps to find him.

1. *Make copies of your dog's photo with his name and your phone number.*
2. *Talk to neighbors and leave a copy of the mini poster with them.*
3. *To entice your dog to come home, place articles of clothing with your scent on them outside your house. Place some of your dog's bedding and some special foods with the clothing.*
4. *Call local veterinarians and emergency clinics in case your dog was injured and taken for treatment.*
5. *Shelters are often required by law to hold dogs for a certain number of days for owners to claim them. Contact shelters in your area in case someone found your dog and turned him over to a shelter. Make daily shelter visits to view the animals yourself; occasionally, shelter staff will not be aware of new animals that have arrived.*
6. *Post flyers of your dog in businesses and shops within a one-mile radius of your home or where he was lost.*
7. *Place an ad in your local newspaper and check the pet lost and found sections daily.*
8. *Call the National Lost Pet Hotline, 900-535-1515, or the National Found Pet Hotline, 800-755-8111.*
9. *Contact the on-line Missing Pets Network, a virtual linking of web sites provided by the U.S. Department of Agriculture, where you can post a notice of a lost pet. In most cases your post will appear on the web site within 24 hours. Visit the page at missingpet.net.*

Hazards Around the House

One of the best ways to ensure your indoor dog's safety is to pet-proof your house. Like child-proofing, pet-proofing is making a clean sweep of every room to which your dog has access and removing or concealing anything that presents a potential danger. Some items may be dangerous to one dog while not to another. For example, electrical cords may be dangerous to the dog that enjoys chewing, but for a dog that isn't into sharpening his teeth on household objects, electrical cords may pose no threat. You may detect other hazards once you've discovered what activities turn your dog on.

• Dogs, especially puppies, love to put things in their mouths just as small children do. Once swallowed, the object of their curiosity can become lodged anywhere along their digestive tract and cause damage. In some cases, surgery may be the only way to remove the offensive item. Keep items small enough to be swallowed out of reach. Such items include rubber bands, coins, paper clips, staples, nails and screws, pieces of string, yarn, thread, or dental floss, earrings and other small jewelry, bells, small balls, sewing needles, pins, and the eyes pets may pull off pet toys.

• Chocolate contains the active ingredient theobromine, which can be toxic to dogs if enough is ingested. It is difficult to estimate how much is required to cause death to a dog because the concentration of theobromine varies with the formulation of the chocolate; milk chocolate will have less theobromine than baker's chocolate, for example. To keep your dog completely safe, do not allow him to eat any chocolate.

• To keep your dog's tags from getting caught in a heating grate when he lies down, place them in a Pet Pocket, which attaches to his collar and lies flat rather than having his tags dangle from a collar.

• To keep your dog from chewing electrical wires, buy plastic decorator shower rod covers and insert the wires inside the rod covers. Rod covers can be cut to size. An alternative for covering electrical wires is to purchase plastic strips designed to conceal wires running across floors, across baseboards, and up walls. Concealing strips are available in hardware or office supply stores. They come in a variety of colors and can be cut to size.

• To protect the pet that likes to chew electrical wires, a newer product to come on the market is the "power strip with a brain" that detects insulation aging, damage, and penetration by such things as dogs' teeth. If your dog tries to take a bite out of this type of cord, the cord will shut off and prevent serious shock. Check your local hardware or builder's supply store.

• If you use an automatic flushing toilet bowl cleaner, put the seat down to keep your dog from drinking the water. Sew a large pom-pom to your toilet seat cover to prevent the lid from staying up in case you forget to lower it.

• Keep chemical cleaning products out of your dog's reach. When possible, substitute nontoxic cleaners such as vinegar and water mixtures and baking soda. Although a Mr. Yuk sticker won't mean anything to Fido, having these stickers (available in pet stores) on dangerous household chemicals might remind you to put them away when finished.

• Human medicines are toxic to animals. Keep them in closed containers out of your dog's reach, and never give him human medicine unless advised to do so by your veterinarian.

• Never give your dog alcoholic beverages. Alcohol can poison your dog.

• Insulation can be hazardous to your dog if he ingests any of it. To protect your dog, keep the insulation contained.

- Ironing boards and irons can easily topple over, hurting the dog sitting underneath. Put both away as soon as you are finished ironing or not in the area to watch him.

- Screen doors and window screens pose a problem to the dog that is propelling himself forward to get at an object of interest outside. Keep all screen doors fastened and screens secure in their sockets.

- Pesticides and bug bait can poison a dog as well as an insect, so keep them out of reach.

- When windows are open during the warm months to let in the summer breezes, keep interior doors blocked with a heavy doorstop to prevent them from slamming shut on your dog.

HOW-TO: Have a Pet-Safe Holiday Tree

Creating a holiday tree that is both beautiful to look at for you and unattractive to your dog is a special challenge. Following are some suggestions to keep your tree pet-friendly.

1. *Tree water at the base of live trees can be harmful if preservative chemicals have been added to prolong the life of the tree. Keep your dog from drinking the water by covering the tree basin with foil or a tree skirt.*
2. *Place dog-safe ornaments near the bottom of the tree in case Rover decides to use the ornaments as playthings.*
3. *Tie up loose electrical cords of the lights used to decorate the tree and keep them concealed by attaching them with wire or cord to the trunk of the tree. End-to-end lights eliminate individual cords dangling from the tree that might entice your dog to chew them.*
4. *If you have lots of tree lights that are not end to end, purchase a power strip in which to plug the lights. Attach the strip to the tree trunk at a level that is higher than the height of your dog. As a result, you will have only one heavy-duty power cord running from the tree to the outlet instead of several flimsy cords from single strings of lights.*
5. *To prevent your dog from knocking over your holiday tree, anchor it with cord or wire to the ceiling directly above the tree's trunk. Don't attach it with wire to a wall behind the tree because your dog could get caught in the wire if he darts behind the tree.*
6. *Spray the lower branches of the tree with bitter apple, cinnamon, lemon, eucalyptus, or other unappealing scents (to your dog) to discourage his curiosity.*

Holiday Safety

Like moving to a new home, surviving the holidays may take some special consideration for the family dog. Lots of visitors who might leave the door open a little too long when they enter or leave, new and unusual gastronomic delights that tempt the dog looking for a quick change in his diet, the presence of decorations that, to most dogs, look like great playthings, or discarded boxes and crumpled wrapping paper that might conceal a puppy or small dog, resulting in his being stepped on, are just a few. To make the end-of-the-year holidays a wonderful time for the two- and four-legged members of your family, follow the suggestions on the next page.

7. Hang your ornaments with ribbons rather than hooks to keep your dog from accidentally swallowing something that could get lodged in his throat.
8. Do not use tinsel or angel hair on your tree. Angel hair, made of glass fiber, and tinsel, made of metal, can cause internal damage if your dog swallows any.
9. Avoid decorating your tree with strings of berries or other edible ornaments—many are harmful if swallowed. The string on which they are attached can cause damage to your dog's intestines if swallowed, and a dog, eager to get to the "treats," could knock over the tree.
10. If you like, decorate a small, artificial tree for your dog with items he will find appealing, such as doggie biscuits and dog toys. Hide the tree until you are ready for your dog to open his presents.

If nothing you do will keep your dog away from your tree, try some of these pet-safe alternatives to trimming a tree:

1. Decorate a mantel or dining room buffet with miniature evergreens or artificial tree boughs trimmed with fruit, nuts, or dried seedpods.
2. Hang a garland above door frames or around picture frames and mirrors.
3. Decorate a two-dimensional tree made from grape vines, rattan, or fake greenery. They are designed to hang from the wall and are available at craft stores.
4. Decorate an outdoor tree. Place on it food items for the birds and squirrels. Your dog will enjoy watching the wildlife.

- If you decorate with candles during the holidays, cover them with glass chimneys to keep Fido from knocking them over and starting a fire.

- Keep a screen in front of your fireplace to keep your dogs out of it or from being burned by flying sparks.

- Several holiday plants are poisonous to pets, such as English holly, Jerusalem cherry, amaryllis, and mistletoe. Keep them out of your dog's reach, or, better yet, don't bring them home. Poinsettias, which have had a bad reputation, are no longer considered toxic.

- Keep poultry bones away from your dog; they can splinter and lodge in his digestive system.

- If guests visit during the holidays, make certain they don't accidentally let your dog out of the house.

- Don't let your dog imbibe any holiday cheer. As little as an ounce of alcohol can poison your dog. Drunken dogs aren't funny, and they may end up dead.

In Case of Emergency

Emergency preparedness is one of those things we deal with to manage the situations we never think we'll have to deal with. Even in the most pet-friendly home or with the most conscientious and caring owner, pets can experience accidents. A knowledge of first aid techniques and a well-stocked emergency kit may make the difference between life and death for your dog. Some of the more common emergencies experienced by dogs include automobile accidents, heatstroke, frostbite, swallowing or attempting to swallow objects, poisoning, electric shock, and other outdoor dangers such as ticks, insect bites, snakebites, porcupine quills, or stepping on sharp objects, so brushing up on restraining techniques and other first aid procedures for these common emergencies may save your dog's life.

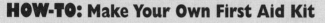

HOW-TO: Make Your Own First Aid Kit

Keep your first aid kit well stocked and replenish items when they dwindle or expire. Label the kit and keep it in a dry, accessible location. Include the following:

- **Tweezers,** *blunt-tipped and pointed for the removal of ticks or objects stuck in your dog's paws or skin*
- *A* **magnifying glass** *to help you see small objects imbedded in wounds or your dog's skin*
- **3% hydrogen peroxide** *for cleaning wounds and scratches*
- **Cotton balls** *and cotton swabs to clean a wound*
- **Antibiotic ointment** *to apply to a wound following cleaning with hydrogen peroxide*
- **Nonstick bandages** *and pads for covering cuts, abrasions, and wounds*
- **Gauze bandages** *(1-inch and 3-inch) to wrap wounds or muzzle panicky dogs that might bite you if excited or in pain. Don't muzzle a dog that is having difficulty breathing. Keep a dog muzzle in your first aid kit*
- **Adhesive tape** *(1-inch) to secure a bandage*
- **Scissors** *to clip the hair around a wound and to cut adhesive tape and bandages*
- **Cardboard** *to make an Elizabethan-style collar to keep a dog from licking his wounds or pulling off the bandages*
- **Clean towels** *and cloths to stop bleeding*
- **Styptic pencil** *to stop bleeding*
- **Pet carrier** *to help carry your dog to your veterinarian*
- **Milk of magnesia** *or* **charcoal tablets** *for poisonings*

The ASPCA/NAPCC recommends the addition of these items to your pet first aid kit so that you can handle an emergency that involves poisons or contamination by a toxic substance:

- **Turkey baster,** *bulb syringe, or large medicine syringe to apply solutions*
- **Saline eye solution** *to flush out eye contaminants*
- *Mild* **grease-cutting dishwashing liquid** *in order to bathe an animal after skin contamination*
- **Rubber gloves** *to prevent you from being exposed to the poisonous agent while you bathe your pet to remove the contaminating substance*

• Keep your veterinarian's phone number near your telephone.

• Know how your veterinarian handles emergency situations after regular business hours. Know the name, telephone number, and location of the nearest veterinary emergency clinic. Keep copies of your dog's medical records, especially if he has a health condition, in the event you must use an emergency clinic.

• Purchase a book on pet first aid and be familiar with basic first aid techniques.

• Have available a first aid kit (see How-to on the previous page). If you prefer, purchase a prepackaged first aid kit designed for dogs. Available at pet stores, first aid kits enable you to keep all necessary first aid items handy in one package. Although more expensive than making your own, prepackaged kits are more convenient.

• Find out if your local Red Cross chapter offers training in first aid for pets and take their course if one is available.

• Know the telephone number and procedures of the ASPCA National Animal Poison Control Center. The ASPCA/NAPCC is a division of the American Society for the Prevention of Cruelty to Animals and is the first animal-oriented poison control center in the United States. The Center is an allied agency of the University of Illinois College of Veterinary Medicine. You may visit their web site for information about the organization at *www.napcc.aspca.org/*, but do not visit the web site when you have a poison-related emergency. You should call your veterinarian or the National Animal Poison Control Center directly.

Incredible Inedible Greens

Your houseplants may be a source of visual pleasure for you, but for the dog that enjoys sinking his teeth into them, houseplants may be a source of danger. Many common houseplants are toxic to pets. Symptoms of ingestion range from nausea, diarrhea, vomiting, and convulsions to death. Not bringing poisonous plants into the home is the best way to protect your dog, but if you have any poisonous plants, keep them out of his reach.

To obtain a complete list of poisonous plants, write to the American Society for the Prevention of Cruelty to Animals/National Animal Poison Control Center (ASPCA/NAPCC), 1717 South Philo Road, Suite #36, Urbana, IL 61802. Enclose a check for $15 payable to NAPCC. The 67-page bound publication is indexed and includes sections for toxic, potentially toxic, and nontoxic plants. It summarizes information from research sources and the ASPCA/NAPCC case database.

Another great source for poisonous plant information is the Cornell University Poisonous Plants web page at *www.ansci.cornell.edu/plants/plants.html/*. The Cornell page includes summaries of the literature and references for each plant, pictures of the plants, the types of poisons present, diagnosis and prevention of animal poisoning, species affected by each plant, and pictures of affected animals. The page also has links to other web pages of toxic plants.

As an alternative, ask your veterinarian for a list of poisonous plants.

Moving Day

Moving to a new home or apartment can be an exciting adventure or an unwanted upheaval. Your dog may view the move exactly as you do, and adjust to the change with little or no effort or with annoyance and anxiety. Generally, older dogs that are more set in their ways and less flexible in their acceptance of change have a more difficult time adjusting to a move to a new home than younger dogs do, so make the change as stress-free for your dog as possible.

• If you are moving to a new apartment or condominium, make certain pets are allowed before taking the leap. If there are "No Pets" rules in effect, consider moving elsewhere rather than giving

up your canine companion. Having to adjust to a new owner—assuming one can be found—will be more traumatic for your dog than adjusting to a new home with you in it.

• If you are having your belongings professionally moved, keep your dogs out of the way. Movers carrying heavy boxes or pieces of furniture will be more concerned about tripping over a pet than they will be about stepping on one. For your dog's safety and that of the movers, crate or leash him on moving or packing day.

• Take your dog to your new home before you move into it so that he can become familiar with the place. Your dog will appreciate being part of the process and will be more comfortable in his new home if he has been given the chance to explore it before making a permanent leap.

The Truth About Antifreeze

Antifreeze will keep your car's engine running in winter, but it may shut down your dog's motor. Because of its sweet taste, antifreeze is appealing to dogs, but if ingested, antifreeze is lethal. Traditionally, antifreeze has been made with ethylene glycol, a highly toxic substance that converts to oxalic acid after ingestion. It damages the kidneys and can cause kidney failure and death. Because of its harmful potential, manufacturers have introduced antifreeze made of propylene glycol instead of ethylene glycol. Prestone's Low Tox and Safe Brands Corporation's Sierra brands are considered pet- and child-friendly. Often, these products are referred to as "safe" or "nontoxic" in spite of the wording on the products' labels. The unfortunate truth is, however, that *no antifreeze,* regardless of its formula, is completely safe. Antifreeze made from propylene glycol is *safer* in that it requires ingesting greater amounts before toxicity occurs, but poisoning and death can result if enough of it is ingested. When dealing with antifreeze, caution is the best strategy. Cleaning up spills and preventing your dog from coming into contact with antifreeze is the best way to protect him from harm no matter which kind of antifreeze you use.

Resources

The ASPCA/National Animal Poison Control Center

Because the ASPCA/NAPCC is a nonprofit organization, a fee is charged in order to offset a portion of the cost of providing the vital service. If you have a poisoning emergency, use one of these telephone options:

Dial 1-800-548-2423 or 1-888-4ANIHELP (1-888-426-4435). The cost for assistance is $45 per case with no extra charge for follow-up calls. You must use Visa, MasterCard, Discover, or American Express when you call. With 800/888 access only, the ASPCA/NAPCC will do as many follow-up calls as necessary in critical cases, and, at the owner's request, will consult his or her veterinarian.

Dial 1-900-680-0000, and the $45 fee per case will appear on your telephone bill. The Center will do as many follow-up calls as necessary in critical cases, and, at the owner's request will contact his or her veterinarian.

When you call the ASPCA/NAPCC, be ready to provide your name, address, and telephone number, any information concerning the exposure to the poison including the type and brand of the poisonous substance, the quantity ingested or contacted, if known, the time since the exposure, the dog's breed, age, sex, and weight, the number of animals involved, and the symptoms your dog is experiencing. For more information, see their web site at *napcc.aspca.org/*.

Keep one of these first aid books handy and familiarize yourself with treating common emergencies:

Hawcroft, Tim. *First Aid for Dogs: The Essential Quick-Reference Guide.* IDG Books, 1994.

Mammato, Bobbie, DVM, MPH. *Pet First Aid: Cats and Dogs.* The American Red Cross and The Humane Society of the United States. Hanover, MD: Mosby Consumer Health and Safety, 1997.

Schwartz, Stefanie. *First Aid for Dogs: An Owner's Guide to a Happy, Healthy Pet.* IDG Books, 1998.

For a heartwarming story of a woman who rescues animals in times of disaster, read:

Crisp, Terri, and Samantha Glen. *Out of Harm's Way.* Pocket Books, 1996.

For stories of animals lost or turned over to shelters, read:

Hess, Elizabeth. *Lost and Found: Dogs, Cats, and Everyday Heroes at a Country Animal Shelter.* Harcourt Brace and Company, 1998.

Lufkin, Elise. *Found Dogs.* IDG Books, 1997.

Papurt, Myrna. *Saved!: A Guide to Success with Your Shelter Dog.* Barron's Educational Series, Inc., 1997.

Feeding Tips

When the hungries hit us, we can choose to pull something out of the refrigerator or head to the nearest restaurant for our meals. Our pets don't have those options. Food that has become stale and moldy or overcome with ants or other bugs, water that has been sitting too long or in the wrong location, and even zits from oily food bowls (see page 44) are some of the food-related problems our dogs may have to face every day. If your dog is trying to tell you something about his eating and drinking options, here are some suggestions for improving his vital victuals.

Armies of Ants

No matter how clean your kitchen is, ants may find it attractive. No matter how careful you are about not dropping bits of food on the floor or not losing them between appliances and furniture cushions, you may find armies of ants marching into your home as though it were a holiday picnic. If you are troubled by ants devouring your dog's food before he does, here are several ways to discourage ants from hitting on your dog's dinner.

• Place your dog's bowls of food inside slightly larger bowls or saucers filled with water. Ants do not swim and will not cross the water to get to the food.

• Purchase one of the new, molded plastic ant-proof bowls that has a saucer to hold water and keep ants at bay.

- Putting your dog's dry food into containers will help keep it fresh and will help keep your neighborhood's ant population from carrying it off.

- Don't leave your dog's uneaten wet food sitting around to attract other bugs. Feed only portions your dog can eat within 20 to 30 minutes, then clean the dish.

- Place containers of dried tansy around your kitchen to keep the ants out. By using tansy as an ant repellent, you won't have to worry about dangerous chemical bug repellents that can be harmful to your dog if he ingests them. Check your local health food or herb store or grow tansy and dry it at the end of the growing season. *A word of caution: Tansy takes over a garden, so it's best to grow it in a pot in a sunny location. Tansy regenerates year after year.*

- To keep armies of ants from devouring your dog's food, find the entry point and sprinkle dried mint or red pepper at the spot.

The Food's Out of the Bag

Dogs are generally not finicky when it comes to dining, but you may find your dog turning his nose up at food that has been sitting around your kitchen, garage, or basement. It could be that his dry food has become stale or moisture laden from sitting around too long. The tasty morsels that made Buster's mouth water when you bought them can lose their flavor and savor because they have become stale and moldy. This is especially true if your home is damp or if you keep your windows open during warm weather. These helpful hints will help keep your dog's taste buds satisfied and your wallet from emptying faster than his container of dry food.

- To keep dry food fresh after opening the container, pour the contents of the bag or box into a plastic or tin airtight container. Store it in a cool, dry place.

- Keeping your dog's dry food away from direct sunlight will help keep it fresh and prevent the oils that are in it from heating up and becoming rancid.

- If you've just bought a big supply of your dog's favorite dry food so you could use up those store coupons before they expired, place some of the food in a container and put it in your freezer, or place the entire bag or box of dry pet food in your freezer if you have room. When it's time to feed it to Buster, get it out of the freezer a few hours ahead of time so it will thaw. Place the unused portion in a sealed container to keep it fresh.

- Newer products, such as the Scoop N Seal, help you keep those large bags sealed tight as the bag empties. Scoop N Seal is available at pet stores.

- Close your dog's bags of dry food with a bag clip. Bag clips come in different sizes for different-sized bags. If you have a home office, perhaps you have some binder clips that will work just as well. Like bag clips, binder clips come in different sizes.

- If you open a bag or box of dry dog food and find it filled with little bugs, chances are that the food expired because it sat in your home or on a grocer's shelf too long. The bug larvae were so tiny that they escaped the food processing equipment and eventually hatched in the food. You will find the expiration date on containers of dry food, so check the dates before purchasing it. If the food has not passed its expiration date when you purchased it, make sure you feed it to your pet before it does.

Gobbling the Greens

No one knows exactly why dogs do it, but they frequently can be seen chomping on grass when they are out for a walk or in their outdoor runs. The habit may be partly instinctive because wild dogs and wolves eat partially or fully digested greens when they feed on a herbivore with a full stomach. Often, dogs swallow the grass whole, and vomit it up soon after. Eating grass may provide some type of nourishment, or the chlorophyll in the grass may provide a stomach-settling remedy, so providing some greens for your dog may aid his digestive process. Make certain that the greens you give your dog are safe.

• Clip off some green grass that is chemical-free and bring it into the house for your dog to eat.

• Keep a container of lettuce in the refrigerator. Cover the lettuce with water. Pour some of the water into a bowl daily for your dog to drink. Replenish the water on the lettuce and return it to the fridge.

• Pour the liquid off steamed or boiled green vegetables. Store it in a container in the refrigerator and pour the liquid over some dry kibble or into a water dish for your dog to drink.

• If you open a can of vegetables, drain the liquid into your dog's water dish or over some dry food.

• Grow some grass in a pot for your dog to nibble on when the spirit moves him.

More than a Meal

With some dogs, meals aren't the only source of oral intake. Wool and other fibers, nondigestible plant material, rubber, plastic, wood, and even their own hair are just some of the things a dog may choose to ingest. Called *pica,* the drive to consume material that is not generally considered food is what animal behaviorists call a compulsive disorder. In a human, a compulsive disorder may be repetitive, such as frequent hand washing or pulling one's hair out. In dogs, these disorders can include excessive licking and spinning in circles. Compulsive disorders are competitive, nonfunctional, nonbeneficial behaviors. Although the exact cause of compulsive disorders is unknown, animal behaviorists feel that they are often caused by stress brought on by environmental conflicts such as competition with other pets, changes in the home, constant punishment, or confinement to small areas such as cages or crates. Lack of socialization or too much attention may bring about a compulsive behavior. A nutritional imbalance can also lead to pica. A dog with a compulsive disorder loses control over his ability to initiate and stop these negative, repetitive actions. Often the compulsive behaviors are oral in nature, causing the dog to eat things he shouldn't.

• The first step in treating a compulsive disorder is to identify the cause and eliminate it. For example, if your dog is crated for a large portion of the day, allow him outside the confined space to help get him on the road to recovery.

• Don't reinforce the behavior by paying attention to him while he is engaged in it. Providing good quality time on a set schedule is preferable and more effective than petting, stroking, or verbally consoling your dog in the midst of repetitive activity.

• Do not reinforce the behavior by punishing your dog for the compulsive behavior or for other inappropriate activities. It may make the problem worse.

• Provide something for your dog to chew on, such as a piece of rawhide.

• Spray household objects your dog likes to chew with cayenne pepper, essential oils in citrus, cinnamon, or eucalyptus scents, spray deodorant, or perfume that is not your own.

• Spray favorite chewables with a pet repellent to deter your dog from sticking non-food objects in his mouth.

• Keep dangerous objects such as yarn or string out of your dog's reach to prevent him from chewing and swallowing them.

• If your dog is chewing his hair, he may have an allergy. Discuss the problem with your veterinarian before embarking on a behavior modification program.

- Add fiber to your dog's diet by mixing vegetables or bran in his food.

- Rub some peanut butter or liver paste on your dog's toys to encourage him to chew on them.

- Soak your dog's rawhide chew in some broth to encourage chewing the rawhide.

- As an alternative, purchase a flavored rawhide chew. Some chews come in bacon or other flavors that appeal to dogs.

- As a last resort to solve a compulsive eating disorder, discuss drug therapy with your veterinarian. Drugs that increase serotonin levels, like Prozac and some antidepressants, are used for treating compulsive disorders, including compulsive eating.

Water, Water Everywhere

...and not a drop to drink. Is evaporation the only reason the water in your dog's water bowl diminishes? Does your dog pester you to drink from a faucet or an outdoor hose? Water is a fundamental building block of nutrition. Without it, dogs, like humans, can become dehydrated and sick. If your dog turns his nose up at his water bowl, here are some suggestions for encouraging him to drink.

- Use separate food and water bowls for your dog instead of dishes that combine the two. Place your dog's water dish away from his food bowl, either in the same room or in another room entirely.

- If your dog likes to drink from the toilet, he may prefer icy cold water to water that is room temperature. Keep a gallon container of water in the fridge and refill your dog's dish two or three times a day.

- As an alternative for the dog that prefers frigid water, place an ice cube or two in his water dish daily.

While the Owner's Away

Does your dog go on a temporary hunger strike while he is boarded or while you are away? Being without the person they are accustomed to or being in a strange environment can cause dogs to feel discomfort and stress that result in a loss of appetite. If you are planning to board your dog or hire a pet-sitter to care for him in your home while you're on a vacation or business trip, here are some suggestions to pass along to keep your dog's digestive juices flowing.

- If you're leaving your dog at home with a pet-sitter, be sure to alert the sitter to the possibility of your dog not eating. A good sitter will ask you for relevant medical information when you sign the pet-sitting contract, but make sure the sitter knows the name and phone number of your dog's veterinarian and how to contact you if an eating or other type of problem develops.

- Along with your dog's regular food, leave some tempting foods such as chicken or turkey to offer him. Keep favorite treats on hand.

- Instruct the sitter to put measured quantities of food in the food bowl so the sitter can tell if your dog is eating. If you use a self-feeder or free-feed, the sitter may not be able to tell how much your dog has eaten.

- Instruct your dog's sitter to hand-feed your dog if he rejects his meals. It may be enough to get him started chowing down.

- Have the sitter take your dog's meal along on his walks. Feeding your dog bits and pieces as he is participating in an enjoyable activity will help entice him to eat.

- If your dog simply wants to sit outside in the yard while leashed, have the bowl of food nearby and periodically offer him food. Like feeding while walking, your dog will associate eating with a pleasant activity.

- Pour gravy or other tasty liquid over dry kibble to make it more appetizing. Leave cans of gravy or broth for that purpose.

- If your dog still won't eat while you are away, you may have a problem. If the dog does not eat for two days, make certain your sitter contacts you or your veterinarian.

Zits

Zits? Yes, believe it or not, dogs can develop them just as a person can. Canine acne can pop up on your dog's face, chin, or lower lip. It appears like small black spots that, if not washed regularly, may turn into crusty patches that cake and bleed. Your dog won't worry about acne preventing him from getting a date, but he may be bothered if the acne builds up. He may try to scratch it off with his toenails, causing the area to bleed and possibly turn raw. While most human acne is limited to the teenagers among the species, canine acne most often occurs in puppies between the ages of three and twelve months. Dogs with oily skin are more susceptible to getting acne than their drier-skinned counterparts, and a dog's food bowl may be part of the problem.

- Keep your dog's chin clean and free of the unsightly blemishes by washing it with a soft cloth and warm water once or twice a day. If the area has begun to bleed, wash it with some hydrogen peroxide on a cotton ball to fight infection.

- A way to help your dog from developing zits or to keep a current case of it from getting worse is to avoid plastic food bowls. Plastic bowls retain oils that add to your dog's acne problem, as his chin rubs against the bowl when he's busy snarfing down dinner. Replace those oil-ridden plastic bowls with aluminum, glass, or lead-free pottery and china bowls.

• Wash your dog's food bowls daily with a mild dish detergent to remove oily deposits.

Resources

Check out some of these books on pet food, feeding, and cooking for your cat or dog:

☞ Dye, Can, and Mark Beckloff. *Three Dog Bakery Cookbook: Over 50 Recipes for All-Natural Paw-Lickin' Treats for Your Dog.* Three Dog Bakery. Kansas City, MO: Andrews McMeel Publishing, 1998.

☞ Palika, Liz. *The Consumer's Guide to Dog Food: What's in Dog Food, Why It's There and How to Choose the Best Food for Your Dog.* IDG Books Worldwide, 1996.

☞ Smith, Cheryl. *Pudgy Pooch, Picky Pooch.* Barron's Educational Series, Inc., 1997.

☞ Visit this America Online web site for information on deciphering pet food labels, pet food ingredients, common terminology, pet nutrition, and much more: *hometown.aol.com/lifegard/petfood/*

Grooming Tips

Dogs as well as dog owners take to the grooming process with varying degrees of acceptance. If your dog balks at a bath or bristles when you wield a brush, the grooming process changes from delight to drudgery. When you adopt a new dog, the time you will have to spend grooming may be a factor in your selection. A Poodle will require more time and effort in the grooming department than a Dalmatian, for example. All dogs require some grooming, but if the time you have to spend is limited, look for a dog with a sleeker, shorter coat that is easier to maintain.

Establish a regular grooming routine and groom your dog at least weekly, or more often if conditions, such as fleas, allergies, romping in the mud, etc., warrant it. Select a place that is convenient for you and have your grooming tools handy. Make the session a positive experience and use treats to reward your dog if you like. If you haven't fixed yourself a cup of chamomile tea as preparation for grooming your dog, reward yourself with a cup of it after you finish the job.

Brushing and Combing

Brushing and combing your dog keep him from developing painful knots that could require the services of a professional groomer to remove. They help you detect the presence of fleas and ticks, and, if combined with a massage, any lumps or bumps in the skin. Brushing and combing your dog also mean that more hair is deposited on your dog's brush or comb and less hair in the environment, resulting in time savings in the cleaning department.

When it comes time to brush up on your dog's grooming, here are some helpful hints.

- Select a brush that is intended for your dog's hair type. Brushes with bristles that are farther apart, such as pin brushes, are useful on dogs with longer, thicker hair, while brushes with shorter, harder bristles are useful on shorthaired dogs.

- If you've purchased your dog from a breeder, ask the breeder what kind of brush is best to use on your breed.

- Wire brushes and slicker brushes help remove dry, dead skin from your dog's coat along with the excess hair. Getting the hair out of the wire brushes and slickers once you've groomed your dog can be difficult if not impossible. To help remove the hair deposits on the wire brush, use a toothpick between the bristles.

- An alternative to a brush is a grooming glove that you wear on your hand. The tiny prongs on the glove's surface remove dead hair as you gently stroke your dog. Pull the hair off for disposal in the trash.

- An undercoat rake will help remove the undercoat of hair on your pet that typically knots up. **Note: *If you are showing your dog, make certain that removing the undercoat of your dog's coat is acceptable for the show ring.***

- To remove excess loose hair from your dog, wrap masking tape around your hand and run the tape lightly over his coat.

- Massage your dog with dampened hands after you take a shower or bath to remove excess hair.

- A damp rubber glove will help remove excess hair from your dog as well as your furniture.

- If your dog enjoys being massaged, purchase a battery-operated massager or one that also functions as a brush and a way to collect loose hair. The gentle sound relaxes tension and the massage soothes sore muscles as you groom your dog.

• Vacuuming hair from your dog helps when shedding season arrives and prevents some of it from attaching itself to your furniture. Some dogs like the vacuum cleaner; others don't. To accustom your dog to the vacuum being gently run over his coat, begin using it when he is a puppy.

• If burrs have become tangled in your dog's hair, crush them with a pair of pliers before brushing them out. Another method of removing burrs is to first saturate them with white petroleum jelly or mineral oil, then work them out of your dog's hair with your hands.

HOW-TO: Clip Your Pet's Claws

Your dog may resort to biting his nails if you don't trim them regularly. How often to clip your dog's nails will depend on the rate at which they grow. Claw clipping should not be an ordeal, although both you and your dog may think so. Following are some time-tested tips when you have to clip your dog's nails.

1. *Scissors can tear the claws, so use only nail clippers designed for use on an animal. The most popular is the guillotine-style into which you insert the claw and squeeze the clipper's handles to cut the nail.*
2. *Use an old laundry bag, towel, or pillowcase to restrain your dog, if necessary. For a small dog, purchase a mini pet straightjacket to keep him under control when you must clip his nails. The device fits snugly and fastens around your dog with velcro. Zippered openings allow you to extend one paw at a time for easy nail clipping.*
3. *Grasp your dog's foot. If he squirms, find someone who can help you hold him steady.*
4. *Slide the clipper onto the nail just below the pink area called the quick.* **Caution: Be certain not to cut above the quick (pink area) of your dog's nails. The quick contains nerves and blood and, when cut, it is very painful to your pet and will result in bleeding. On some dogs the quick is difficult to see because they have dark nails. As a rule of thumb, cut your dog's nails just beyond the point where the nail begins to curve. If you are not sure, ask your veterinarian to show you.**
5. *Squeeze the clippers to clip off the nail tip with one smooth action.*
6. *If you accidentally cut through the quick and your dog's nail bleeds, stop the bleeding by holding a clean cloth or cotton swab to the nail or by applying a little styptic powder, a moistened styptic pencil, or dipping the nail in some flour to stop the bleeding. If bleeding persists, take your dog to a veterinarian.*

• Thinning shears will help you thin your dog's hair during warmer seasons, and they are useful when you must remove knots from his coat. **Note: If you are showing your dog, make certain that thinning your dog's hair is acceptable for the show ring.**

• If your local pet store doesn't have the right brush or comb for your dog, visit a pet grooming supply store or a dog show, or order them through one of the mail-order catalogs or from an Internet pet store listed in the last chapter of this book.

• When brushing and combing your dog, check the skin for signs of dermatitis or parasites. If you detect any problems, see your veterinarian.

Controlling Fleas and Ticks

Summertime, and the livin' is easy for the tiny insects that love to feed off your dog. If you see one flea on your dog, you will see hundreds within a week. If you're less than lucky, you also may see the products of their reproductive cycles in the form of eggs they hatch before your very eyes in a warm spot, such as where your dog sleeps. Ticks, on the other hand, may attach themselves to your dog and go unnoticed until they embed in his skin and potentially cause some real damage. If you live in a warm, humid region of the country, your dog is more inclined to experience flea and tick infestations than if you live in a cooler, drier climate.

Battling these external parasites has become a lot easier in recent years with the development of new flea- and tick-fighting products, but the best way to ensure that your dog and you don't become overrun by fleas and ticks is to never let your guard down. Check your dog's coat after every romp in the outdoors during flea and tick season and keep him armed against these pesky critters. The most common areas of an animal in which you will notice fleas is around the neck, behind the ears, and at the base of the tail. Flecks of flea feces and eggs that look like salt and pepper fall off an infested dog and are deposited wherever he sits or sleeps. Ticks can land anywhere on your dog, so be sure to brush out his coat after a walk.

If you do get a flea infestation, you must eliminate them from your dog and your home. Adult fleas as well as the eggs and larvae *must* be destroyed.

• "The best offense is a good defense" goes the old football adage, but it is also true when it comes to flea-fighting products. Ask your veterinarian for information on the flea buster in pill or liquid form, Program or the topicals—Frontline, Revolution, or Advantage—for the most effective way to prevent fleas from attacking your dog. Developed to kill flea eggs and larvae as well as adult fleas, these products are the most effective and efficient ways to prevent flea infestations before they start.

• If you are using flea shampoo to rid your dog of fleas, lather a ring of suds around his neck when starting to bathe him to keep fleas from running up to his head.

• Flea combs trap fleas in the metal teeth for removal and disposal.

• Another way to pick fleas off your dog is to first dab your finger in petroleum jelly.

• To get fleas out of your carpet and keep the larvae from hatching, sprinkle the carpet with table salt or borax. Allow to stand for several hours, then vacuum.

• When vacuuming during a flea infestation, throw away the vacuum cleaner bag after each use to prevent any eggs or larvae you've picked up from hatching.

• If you use a fogger or inverted aerosol spray to remove fleas from your home, make sure it has an insect growth regulator (IGR) to kill fleas in all of their life stages.

- To remove ticks, use a blunt-tipped pair of tweezers. Put the tick in a plastic bag and take it to your veterinarian for analysis of what type of tick it is and discuss Lyme disease potential.

- As an alternative, purchase a tool specifically designed to remove ticks. The tool can be carried on a key ring or attached to a jacket zipper for quick access on those hikes through the woods.

Dousing the Dog

These days, dog washes are as much a ritual as car washes, and it's not uncommon to be driving along and see signs for a dog wash sponsored by a local nonprofit group. Some dogs were bred to be comfortable in water, but others need a little coaxing to get a hose-down. The tips below will help you get the water onto your dog and your dog into the water.

- Sometimes, getting a job done is as simple as having the right tools, and bathing your dog is no exception. An indoor pet spray that attaches to your sink faucet or showerhead makes bathing your dog easier to manage. The spray is gentle enough for a small dog.

- If you must bathe your dog indoors, getting him into the tub may be a job in itself, let alone bathing him once he's there. To help in the effort, purchase a dog bath helper that has a mini lead attached to a suction cup that sticks to the bottom or side of the tub. The suction cup can be easily removed once your dog is squeaky clean.

- When rinsing the soap from your dog's coat, use a one part vinegar to four parts water solution to leave his coat shiny and clean.

- If your dog just doesn't like the water, use a *waterless* shampoo that must be applied then lathered into his coat until a foam appears. Brush and towel-dry with a blow-dryer.

- If you prefer, give your dog a dry bath to remove any odors when it's too cold to bathe him. Rub some baking soda into your dog's coat, gently massage it in, then brush it out.

- To help give a small dog a bath, place a small window screen across the sink in which you want to bathe him. The screen will give your dog something to stand on, and, because the bath and rinse water flow beneath it, will prevent him from having to stand in water.

- If your small dog struggles when it's bath time, try the Bathe N' Carry device that combines a solid base with a wire cage secure enough to hold dogs up to 20 pounds (9 kg) steady but with openings large enough for you to insert your hands to shampoo and rinse him.

- If you want to give your dog some extra help in the self-cleaning department but don't want to stress him by subjecting him to a bath, use pet cleansing wipes to remove dander and saliva from his coat. The product, made from all-natural ingredients, leaves your dog's coat clean and healthy looking.

- If your dog comes into contact with chewing gum, remove it by rubbing an ice cube on the gum until it hardens and can be pulled out, then wash the area thoroughly.

- If your dog walks on tar, remove it by rubbing butter or margarine on the tarred area until the tar softens and can be pulled off. Repeat if necessary, then bathe your dog's feet.

- If your dog rubs against oil-based paint, wipe it off immediately with a dry cloth, then bathe him. If the paint has dried and hardened, cut it out, then bathe your dog. *Caution: Do not use paint remover, kerosene, turpentine, or gasoline to remove paint from your dog's hair.*

- If your dog doesn't like the sound of spray conditioner after his bath, spray the conditioner on a brush, then run the brush through his hair.

The Pearly Whites

A pretty smile may not be on your dog's priority list, but having sound teeth to chew his food certainly is. Your veterinarian will examine your dog's teeth as part of his annual checkup, but don't wait until a yearly exam to help prevent your dog from developing dental disease. Tartar and plaque can form on your dog's teeth as they can on your own, and tooth loss and gum disease can just as easily develop. Some dental problems may be a result of genetic manipulation and breeding. Some miniature dogs, for example, may have tooth problems from birth due to having the same number of teeth as a large dog being crammed into their smaller jaws. Other dogs develop dental problems as they age. Whatever the cause, help your dog in the dental department by cleaning his teeth twice weekly and following some of these suggestions.

• Accustom your dog to having his teeth cleaned early in life. Make the session a game and reward your dog with a tartar-control treat.

• Two types of teeth-cleaning products exist that fit over the pet owner's fingertips. One is a rubber device a little larger than a thimble with tiny rubber spikes on it. The other has an actual brush on it so that you can brush your dog's teeth, *using only toothpaste that is intended for dogs.* The brush can be sterilized in a microwave oven after each use.

• If you prefer to use an actual brush, use a soft toothbrush meant for a baby.

• If your dog has a very small mouth, use a human eyebrow brush.

• Try a little baking soda instead of pet toothpaste to clean your dog's teeth. ***Caution: Human toothpaste is intended to be spit out and will make your dog sick if he swallows it.***

- An alternative way to clean your dog's teeth is to rub them several times a week with a dampened terrycloth washcloth. To make it more enjoyable for your dog, rub a little garlic on the cloth.

- If your dog runs in the other direction when he sees you whip out the toothbrush and paste, offer him treats or food products that are designed to remove plaque and prevent the buildup of tartar. Give him some hard, dry, crunchy food as a part of his normal diet to help clean plaque deposits. Manufacturers have developed foods and treats to reduce the amount of tartar and plaque. Most are available in grocery stores and supermarkets.

- Discuss with your veterinarian having your dog's teeth cleaned professionally. Teeth cleaning requires that your dog be anesthetized.

- If your dog has poorly aligned teeth, orthodontic appliances are a possibility. Discuss options with your veterinarian.

- If your dog has bad breath, it could signal the sign of disease. Have your dog checked by a veterinarian. To help reduce bad doggie breath, purchase products intended to make your dog's breath smell better. They are available at pet stores.

- As an alternative way to improve your dog's breath, mix three parts water to one part non-mint liquid chlorophyl (available in health food stores) in a medicine bottle. Liquid chlorophyl is a natural deodorant. Give your dog one dropperful daily to fight bad breath from the inside.

Stifling the Stinks

If your dog comes into contact with a skunk, aromatherapy will take on a whole new meaning. If your dog is not allowed to run free, chances are he will never come face to face, or face to rear, with a skunk, but if he meets one of these cute but smelly creatures head on, here are some remedies for removing the skunk's lingering, musky odor from his coat.

• A good remedy for removing skunk odor is to wash your dog with tomato juice followed by a bath using dog shampoo and water. Rinse your dog with water and lemon juice or vinegar.

• Try a pet-safe odor neutralizer that can be used to bathe your dog. Read directions carefully to make certain the product can be used to bathe your dog.

Resources

Try some of these helpful books before taking the grooming plunge with your pet:

Ballner, Maryjean. *Dog Massage.* St. Martin's Press, 2000.

Buckle, Jane. *How to Massage Your Dog.* Howell Book House, 1995.

Fenger, Diane, Arlene F. Steinle, and William Watson Denlinger. *The Standard Book of Dog Grooming.* Alpine Publications, 1996.

Pinney, Christopher. *Guide to Home Pet Grooming.* Barron's Educational Series, Inc., 1990.

If you prefer to see how it's done rather than read about it, watch this video:

Lane, Ena. *Show Off Your Dog: Grooming Basics.* MJM /A.R.T. Productions, VHS Tape. A.R.T. Productions, 1997.

Behavior Tips

Dogs, although domesticated for thousands of years, bring with them some of the behaviors that are found in their wild ancestors. When domestic dogs are forced to live in the wild, these behaviors help them survive. In our homes, the same behaviors range from moderately cute to annoying or even dangerous. Behavior problems are one of the major reasons pets are relinquished to shelters or euthanized by veterinarians. Aggression, biting, and urine marking are just a few of these undesirable behaviors. If your good efforts can't solve a behavior problem, seeking professional help in the form of a certified animal behaviorist may be the next step.

Anxious Animals

Four-legged animals are as inclined to experience stress as their two-legged owners. While your dog won't labor over where his next meal will come from, he may wrestle with his own fears and anxieties. Fear may be associated with a particular person or gender, or a specific situation, such as a visit to the veterinarian's office. Dogs may become anxious when their owners are away, when they hear certain noises such as thunder or fireworks, when a new pet enters the house or an animal companion dies. Eliminating the cause is the first step in preventing your dog's anxiety attacks. If your dog runs under the bed during a thunderstorm, the source of the stress is clear, but sometimes the cause of the stress is more difficult to determine. To help a nervous pet, try some of these tension-easing tips.

• If your dog has a fear of thunder or fireworks, desensitizing your pet is almost impossible. Instead, provide a place in your home away from windows and doors in which he can wait out the storm and keep a radio on to help drown out the sounds of the thunder or fireworks.

• If your dog experiences anxiety over a new pet addition to the home, introduce the animals gradually (see the section called "Happy to Meet You" on page 65, which describes how to introduce pets to one another).

• Dogs may experience stress at being left alone. Consider the option of adopting or purchasing a second dog to keep your existing dog company.

• If your dog seems anxious when you are away even for short periods of time, leave the television or a radio on.

• If your dog becomes stressed because you are moving to a new home, take him to your new home before you move in, if possible, and allow him to investigate the surroundings. Give your dog some treats or play with him in the new home so he will associate something positive with the experience.

• If the appearance of a new baby or new spouse in your home is making your dog anxious, try to keep things as normal as possible. Stick to your dog's regular schedule and give him plenty of attention.

• If your dog grieves due to the loss of an animal companion, give him plenty of love and affection. After some time passes, consider a new animal playmate.

• If your dog develops severe anxieties that cannot be solved with behavior modification techniques, discuss drug options with your veterinarian. Calming drugs may be the only way to help some animals overcome their anxieties.

• If you must walk your dog or allow him to go outside when fireworks are going off, keep him leashed and under your control at all times to prevent him from bolting loose. Allow your dog to be outside only when necessary during the fireworks.

HOW-TO: Accustom a Dog to Being Alone

If your dog has trouble dealing with your absence, as evidenced by chewing and other destructive behaviors, a program of desensitization will help him learn how to be alone. Over time, you can leave your dog for longer and longer periods without the onset of anxiety from your absence.

Be patient and apply the techniques below gradually. It may take days or weeks until your dog stops being anxious when you leave him alone. If your dog has reverted to old habits or is not learning as fast as you are applying the techniques, go back to square one and begin the program again. Practice the sessions daily.

Note: Physical punishment may cause the dog to seek other means of satisfying his urges and to come to distrust you, so reproof your pooch without a heavy hand.

1. *Teach your dog how to sit and stay (see the section on obedience, page 67). Practice these commands as you move farther away from him, increasing the distance from a few steps to another room of the house. Praise your dog for obeying the command.*
2. *After you have determined that your dog will stay when you go into another room, go to and from the front door using the sit and stay commands. If your dog obeys, praise him and offer him a treat.*
3. *Choose a phrase to use when exiting your home, such as "I'll be right back." Use that phrase every time you go out the door.*
4. *Gradually accustom your dog to being left alone for seconds, then increase the time you are gone to several minutes. If your dog seems relaxed, lengthen the time you are outside during your training sessions. If your dog appears anxious, keep the sessions to one or two minutes until he calms down.*
5. *As a last resort for the dog that cannot cope with being alone, discuss anti-anxiety medication with your veterinarian.*

Attack Dog on Duty

Aggression in dogs may be associated with fear, establishing, controlling, and protecting territories both inside and outside the home, dominance, object guarding, psychoses, relationships with others of the same species, play, or feeling pain. Dogs become aggressive because they feel threatened, whether the threat is real or only imagined. They will use the only weapons they have at their disposal—their teeth and bodies—to ward off the potential danger. Signs of aggression vary depending on the cause, but an aggressive dog may stare, lower his head, stalk, growl, bark, show his teeth, and, in the extreme, attack and bite. A mildly aggressive dog may simply jump on people or pull on his leash when walked.

Most dogs exhibit some types of aggression periodically. Aggression is one of the ways they communicate, and a certain amount of it is natural between members of the same species. When the aggression becomes commonplace or threatens household members, including other pets, the behavior is a problem. As with all behavior problems, prevention is the best cure. Even if you live with a mild-mannered wimp, your dog may develop aggressive tendencies that are a result of environmental factors or his physical condition as he ages. Here are some tips for dealing with an attack dog.

• If your previously peaceable dog shows signs of aggression, have him examined by a veterinarian to make certain there is nothing physical causing him to behave aggressively. Your dog may have a medical problem that causes him to experience pain when you pet or lift him, for example.

• Check your environment to determine if anything is causing your dog to be aggressive. For example, is anyone in the home teasing your dog? When your dog goes outside into his fenced yard, are any neighborhood children tormenting him? If the source of your dog's aggression is environmental, eliminate the source of the problem.

- If you've eliminated physical and environmental factors as a source of the aggressive behavior, nip the problem in the bud. Whatever training technique you use, practice it consistently and immediately. Waiting an hour after your dog has conducted himself aggressively to correct the behavior won't have any effect.

- Punishment should *never* be physical—your intent is to startle your dog and disrupt his behavior.

- Staring is threatening behavior for dogs. Avoid staring at your dog, especially if he appears defensive. When looking at or gazing at your dog, blink slowly every few seconds. Blinking allows mutual gazing without threat.

- Don't take chances on being hurt by an aggressive dog. If your dog is threatening, appears dangerous, and possibly injurious, consult a professional behaviorist. A behaviorist will outline a plan to correct the situation based on your dog, the type of aggression, and the source of the problem.

- Poor breeding can be a cause of aggression in dogs. Before buying that pedigreed pooch, visit the kennel and breeder to check out the conditions under which the dog was raised. Avoid buying a dog from a pet store because you will never be able to investigate his background.

- Some animal behaviorists and experts recommend avoiding certain breeds because they may require more attention and effort in training. Since Rottweilers, Pit Bulls, and German Shepherd Dogs have been given a bad rap as being aggressive and dangerous, avoid these breeds if you've never owned a dog and lack experience handling them.

- If your dog is aggressive about food, place some treats in a plastic container and shake it. If your dog growls at being interrupted while eating or at being offered food, shake the container and throw your dog a treat. Continue this process until your dog associates the shaking with being offered a treat and allows interruptions to his feeding regimen.

• If your dog barks at strangers or visitors approaching the house, use the treats in a container method to make him associate visitors with something positive rather than threatening. Have the guest give your dog the treats.

• If someone your dog finds objectionable visits you regularly, or if you must have your protective dog cared for by a neighbor or pet-sitter, have the person leave an article of clothing he or she has worn. Place the clothing where your dog likes to sleep so that he can become accustomed to the person's scent, associate it with something pleasant, and recognize the person when he or she shows up.

• Teach your dog verbal commands such as "Sit" and "Stay" as a way of stopping aggressiveness in certain situations, such as aggressiveness related to food and being fed.

• Avoid playing games that entice your dog to attack other animals or perhaps children. If you are unsure how your dog will react to other animals, keep him leashed and under your control in the presence of other pets.

Biting the Hand That Feeds

You may think the game you are playing with Fido is fun, but your dog may think otherwise. As a general rule, dogs bite because, from the dog's perspective, the person bitten presented a potential threat or was engaging in conduct that the dog found objectionable. Dogs that bite for no apparent reason are most often motivated by their upbringing or training. It is a sad comment in present-day American society that the pet that was once considered man's best friend is becoming man's worst enemy. Dog bites are a common problem these days. The Centers for Disease Control calculates that since 1979 there have been more than five million reported dog bites in the United States, with almost one million of them requiring medical attention. The CDC estimates that many more dog bites go unreported. Twenty out of every twenty-five bites are sustained by children, and many of them involve being bitten by the family pet. To prevent your pooch from biting the hand that feeds him, follow these suggestions.

• If you are planning to purchase or adopt a dog and you have young children in the house, train the children early how to approach and handle the dog. Dogs that are chased, tormented, or teased in what the kids perceive as fun are the ones that are most likely to attack when they've had enough.

• Learn to recognize pre-attack body language and stop interacting with your dog immediately, even if you feel that what you are doing is not offensive. Your dog may feel otherwise.

• Don't play aggressive games with your dog. Dogs taught to attack an inanimate object in what is thought to be harmless play will soon transfer what they have learned to living beings.

• Provide your dog with obedience training when he is young so that he will obey your commands to stop what he is doing in the event he attempts to go after you, another person, or an animal.

• Unless you really need an attack dog, don't protection-train him. Your dog will scare off potential intruders by barking, so providing him with attack training will be like leaving a loaded gun where anyone can use it.

• Consider placing a muzzle on your aggressively inclined dog when you are walking him or when he is in other social situations to prevent him from biting someone.

Chewing

Does your dog seem to have an oral fixation? Does he want to put things in his mouth that he shouldn't? Dogs chew objects for a variety of reasons. Puppies chew because they are teething. When an owner, family member, or other pet is gone, chewing may become a compulsive behavior due to separation anxiety. If your dog's chewing is gnawing at your nerves, follow some of the suggestions below to curb the crunching.

• Whenever possible, keep objects away from your dog that he finds fun to chew, whether it be your freshly washed socks, pieces of string, or ribbon from packages or gifts.

• Spray bitter apple on objects, such as electrical cords, to prevent your dog from sinking his teeth into them.

• Rub favorite objects with scented oils that are unappealing to your dog, such as eucalyptus, cinnamon, or citrus.

• Spray a cologne that is not your scent onto objects to dissuade the chewer.

• If your dog is teething, offer him a variety of chew toys and direct his attention to them when you observe him chewing something he shouldn't.

• Crate or kennel training may be the solution for a dog that chews on objects while his owner is away. Placing your dog in a crate while you are at work may save your home from being chewed up. Place your dog's belongings, food, and water in the crate so that he will feel secure. Have a friend, neighbor, or pet-sitter walk and play with your pooch midday to give him some exercise.

• If your dog engages in destructive chewing, especially if the target is a part of his own body, it could be a sign of boredom. Schedule regular play sessions each day so that your dog will anticipate them. Take your dog on regular walks instead of just letting him outside on a chain or in an enclosed yard to find something to do on his own. Make sure he has your complete attention during the play sessions and does not have to share you with the telephone, the television, or other disturbances around the house or around the neighborhood.

Fighting Like Cats and Dogs

Put two or more people under the same roof, and tensions occasionally flare up. If two people can't always keep the lid on emotional outbreaks, why should pets be expected to do so? Naturally, your pets will have a spat periodically. After all, they are often the only ones that know what circumstances brought it about. If one animal appears to be in danger from another, breaking up the brawl may be necessary. If your canine housemates get into a squabble, try some of these methods to separate the animals without risking your own life or limbs.

• Reproductive drives can be a source of fighting, especially among males, so spaying or neutering your dogs will reduce outbreaks as a result of biological urges.

• Proper introductions and training will go a long way in preventing fights before they start. For details on how to introduce pets, see the section called "Happy to Meet You" (page 65) in this chapter.

noogie noogie

• Water is one of the most effective and most harmless ways to separate two dogs that have locked horns. If the dogs are outside, squirt them with a hose. If indoors, squirt them with a squirt bottle or grab the nearest plastic container and fill it with water to douse the two.

• Give your dogs their own food dishes, beds, and toys to discourage competition that may cause them to fight.

• Forming a hierarchy is natural to dogs. To keep your dogs from fighting, respect the hierarchy. Feed the alpha (dominant) dog first and don't give the dogs lower on the hierarchy special attention or favors in order to keep the hierarchy stable.

- Try grabbing the dogs' collars to pull them apart. If you can't get to the collar without risk of teeth marks in your hands, try another method.

- Some behaviorists recommend grabbing one dog's legs and lifting them up and away from the other dog. Be careful not to yank or pull so hard as to tear a muscle or injure the dog's hips or legs.

- Use a pepper spray product that is formulated for dogs. The product will get the two dogs to stop fighting before they injure each other. *Caution: Do not spray into the dog's eyes!*

- Try maneuvering the dogs into a doorway and separate them with the door.

Happy to Meet You

If you have a resident dog and want to adopt a cat, the good news is that the two have a great chance of getting along. The bad news is that temperaments of individual animals vary, so see the tips below to determine if your dog will be receptive to a companion of another species.

Adopting or purchasing a dog known to get along with another species will save you time and energy helping each adjust to the other. A dog exposed to cats some time in his past is more likely to get along with a newcomer brought into the home, assuming the exposure was a positive one. If you obtained your dog at a shelter, ask the shelter staff if they know anything about his history and whether he came from a home that had both dogs and cats. If you purchase your dog from a breeder, inquire what other kinds of pets the breeder has. If you don't know ahead of time, try some of these techniques for identifying a cat-friendly dog.

- If your dog wants to chase small animals he sees when he is outside or on a walk, bringing home a cat or a kitten would be a mistake.

• If your dog enjoys pleasing you and other people, he is more likely to do well when he knows you want him to accept the cat.

• If your dog understands rudimentary behavioral commands and obeys them, you will have a better chance of establishing a successful relationship with a new cat.

• Some of the more aggressive or active breeds of dogs may be a potential hazard to a cat and especially to a kitten. If your dog is a terrier or a sighthound bred to chase smaller animals, he may have a difficult time containing himself around a playful kitten.

HOW-TO: Introduce Dogs to Cats

Following some basic guidelines will help your dog and new cat get off on the right paw.

1. *Isolate the cat in a separate room for a week or more. If no room is available for her, use a crate big enough for the cat, food and water bowls, toys, and a litterbox. Put the crate in a private location that is away from the hustle and bustle of the house.*
2. *Spend time interacting with the cat so that she gets to know you and feel comfortable in your presence.*
3. *Spend time with your dog so that he does not feel he is being abandoned or his territory is being invaded by a new pet.*
4. *Don't hurry the introduction process. Your pets will be spending their days together for a long time, so be prepared to spend a few weeks, or even months, if necessary, making certain the introductions work.*
5. *Never force the introductions. Don't take a kitten or cat to the resident dog. Holding them up to one another before they are ready can cause irreparable harm and prevent the two animals from ever liking each other.*
6. *Feed both animals on either side of the door to the room in which the cat is isolated so that they can associate something positive with each other's presence.*
7. *Prior to face-to-face meetings, rub each of the animals with a towel that has been rubbed over the other to familiarize each with the other's scent.*
8. *Once the cat is comfortable with you and her room, confine your dog in the cat's room and allow the cat to explore the rest of the house for brief periods of time up to an hour or so. Your dog will be able*

Obeying Your Commands

Imagine that you or another household member held a door open too long and your dog, seeing an opportunity for a neighborhood escapade, escaped before you had a chance to stop him. This and a thousand other scenarios are good reasons to give your dog the rudiments of obedience training. If your dog understand the commands *sit, stay, come,* and *down,* you may prevent an accident from befalling your beloved animal companion and reduce the stress both of you feel when your dog doesn't listen. Once your dog has mastered the basics, the sky's the limit for teaching him lots of other instructions or tricks. Your dog will enjoy learning the commands and will want to please you.

to learn about the cat by scent while he is confined in the cat's room. While the cat explores your house, spend time with your resident dog so that he continues to feel that the cat poses no threat.

9. When your new cat appears comfortable in the house, conduct the first face-to-face meeting. Keep your dog leashed and allow the cat to come to the dog. Talk to both in a calm voice. Offer both of them treats.

10. If your dog is interested but not aggressive, allow him to examine the cat. If your dog appears too eager, give the leash a gentle tug and command your dog to sit or stay. Continue allowing both pets to meet on a limited basis until you are confident that your dog recognizes the cat as a member of your family. **Caution: If you're bringing home a kitten, never allow her to be alone with an adult dog; because your kitten is small, she could be hurt easily if not intentionally.**

11. Give the two animals constant supervision during initial face-to-face meetings and observe them closely to determine when to give them the space to become better acquainted.

12. Allow the animals to have an occasional spat as long as neither is in danger. A dog's playful bark may alarm a cat the first time she hears it, but the cat will soon learn what it means. A cat's swat of annoyance at a dog that is overly eager may sting the first time, but the dog will soon learn not to be too gregarious in the cat's presence.

13. During the introductory process, provide each pet with a place to go that is off-limits to the other so that he or she can feel comfortable and safe.

The clicker

One of the hottest training methods these days uses a nifty, ingenious gadget called a clicker. A clicker is a small metal device or child's cricket that has a piece of spring steel attached that makes a clicking sound when pressed. Initially accompanied by a positive reinforcement, such as food, clickers reinforce the reward during training until the sound of the clicker itself becomes the reinforcer for good behavior. Such associations are called *secondary reinforce-*

HOW-TO: Clicker-Train Your Pet

Before beginning to teach basic commands, set up your sessions by following these steps:

1. *Always be in a good mood when conducting training sessions. If you are not, your dog will pick up on your negative emotions and associate them with the commands, resulting in less inclination to obey them.*
2. *Keep sessions short, about ten or fifteen minutes at a time, to keep your dog or you from becoming bored or frustrated.*
3. *Be consistent with the commands you use. Don't use a word or phrase for a command during one session and change it the next time for the same activity. Changing your commands will only confuse your dog. Keep the commands to one word preferably or a maximum of two, such as "Get down."*
4. *Select as the food reward something that is extra appealing to your dog so it functions as a motivator.*
5. *Conduct training sessions prior to regular meals so that your dog is hungry and more apt to perform for the food reward—but don't starve your dog to train him.*
6. *Train your dog in a location that is free of distractions, and give the process your complete attention. While watching your favorite television show may be a good time to use the exercycle, it's not a good time to train your dog. Eventually you will want your dog to obey commands when he is outside. Begin teaching the basics indoors or in an enclosed outdoor area, however, until you are sure that your dog has learned to obey to you.*
7. *Use your dog's name along with the command you are trying to teach ("Fido, sit"). In addition to the food reward, praise your dog when he performs the behavior you desire.*
8. *Always have your clicker and food reward on hand when you begin your session. If you can't obtain a clicker, use another device such as a small plastic container of treats that you rattle, two spoons that you click together, or even clucking your tongue. Just make sure that whatever you use, you keep it consistent. Starting with one device then changing to another later on means you will have to start training from the beginning again.*

ment and have been in use in animal training for many years. They are even in use in the home now. When you get out your dog's leash, he gets excited because he knows he is going for a walk. When you open the jar of doggie biscuits, he comes running. The sight of the leash and the sound of the jar opening act as reinforcement for a desired activity. In the same way, the sound of the clicker acts as reinforcement because your dog will associate it with a primary reward stimulus, such as food.

9. Always click the clicker at the moment your dog is performing the behavior you want.

10. Before beginning to train your dog, make the clicking sound when you feed him his regular meals or when you offer a treat so he begins to associate the sound with eating. After you have done this for a week or so, go to your dog's regular feeding station and make the clicking sound. If he comes running, he has associated the sound of the clicker with being fed. Now you can begin the specific training. Be sure to offer food on this occasion so he continues to make the connection.

Sit

1. With your dog in front of you facing in your direction, let him smell the food, then slowly move the food reward back and over his head. As your dog's head follows the food, he will naturally sit down. Make the clicking sound and offer the food reward immediately. Continue the process.

2. Once your dog learns the behavior, give it a name, such as "Sit." Soon your dog will begin to associate the food reward with the command, and you will no longer have to use the clicker to make him sit. Simply saying "Sit" will be enough.

Come

1. Now that you've already trained your dog to come to his food bowl at the sound of the clicker, you can begin to associate the command, "Come," with the behavior. Say your dog's name, hit the clicker, and say "Come."

2. When your dog comes to the food station, offer a treat. Try using the same technique from other locations around the house. When your dog comes, hit the clicker a few times and praise him. Give your dog the food reward immediately. Gradually, just say "Come" to call your dog.

You can use these same techniques to teach your dog other commands like "Down" or "Stay."

Housebreaking

Even though your dog will determine *when* he has to relieve himself, *where* he relieves himself should be your choice for the most part. Theories abound on the best way to housebreak a puppy. For more detailed information about the process, check out some of the resources listed at the end of this chapter. Below are some suggestions from other dog owners who have added their own brand of expertise to the housebreaking process.

• Crating your puppy is a good way to prevent him from urinating indoors. The crate becomes the puppy's home when you are not there, and theoretically your puppy will be hesitant about soiling his own space. Provide your puppy with bedding and a chew toy in the crate. Exercise your puppy and take him for a walk to do his business before placing him in the crate.

• Instead of a crate, use an old playpen or puppy playpen with a shower curtain, drop cloth, or thick towel on the bottom as a way to train your puppy. Put lots of newspapers on the bottom over the shower curtain, cloth, or towel. When you take your puppy for a walk, take some soiled newspaper with you so your puppy gets the idea of what he is supposed to do.

• Use baby gates to confine your puppy to specific rooms or areas of the house to keep puppy and soiled spots confined.

• If your puppy is not crated, place potty pads over newspaper by the door or in specific locations where your puppy potties to absorb moisture. (Absorbent pads are available in pet stores.)

• Always take your puppy out through the same door so he learns to go to that door when he must relieve himself.

"Urine" My Territory

As with humans, vocalizing comprises only a small percentage of the ways dogs communicate. Barking, growling, and snarling are just a few of the ways your dog will let you or another animal know how he feels. Reading a dog's mind can be as easy as reading his body language, so knowing the meaning of signals such as tail wagging or teeth baring is an important step toward understanding what your dog is telling you. One of the ways dogs communicate with other dogs is through scent marking. You may never fathom the subtleties of communication by scent. Scent markers provide some geographic orientation so that the dog can identify the space as being inhabited by another pack or individual. If the dog is lost, scent markers help him find his way home. Scent marking also helps a dog to be more comfortable and self-assured about where he is. This is apparent when a dog begins to mark indoor locations when the owner moves to a new house. Finally, dogs may engage in allo-marking—marking other members of the pack—to give them a common smell for the purposes of identification. When a dog marks his owner, he is saying "You are an accepted member of my animal family."

Scent marking is a natural behavior. The sense of smell is highly developed in dogs, and your dog will pick up the odor and react accordingly. Scent marks result when an animal rubs against an object or when he digs. The most common form of scent marking, however, is achieved when a dog sprays urine. Although spraying to mark territory is a behavior commonly associated with male dogs, females also spray. A dog that exhibits marking behavior will sniff the spot, lift his leg or squat, and squirt a bit of urine onto the surface. Dogs leave these scent markers for any future canine travelers to smell. Inside your home, dogs may scent mark territories, particularly if there is more than one pet in the house-

hold. Even the presence of dogs outside the home may elicit the urine-marking behavior from the indoor pet. Try these steps to impede your dog's urine-marking impulses.

• The best way to stop urine marking before it starts is to have your dog neutered or spayed. Urine marking is more prevalent among sexually intact and active members of the species, so altering will help remove the drive. Veterinarians are spaying and neutering pets at an earlier age, so discuss with your veterinarian the possibility of altering your dog soon after you adopt him.

• Drug therapy may help a spraying dog, particularly if the dog dribbles or marks due to fears and anxieties. Eliminating the source of the anxiety is the first step to solving the problem, but you may want to discuss drug alternatives with your veterinarian if a behavior modification program does not work.

• Change the function of the spot marked by placing your dog's food bowls at the location.

• If a particular spot in your home is attractive to your dog, keep him away from the area altogether.

• If your dog marks locations around the neighborhood while you are walking, allow him to engage in the marking behavior. Marking outdoors is harmless and will give your pooch a sense that all is right with the world.

Resources

For further reading, try some of these general books on cat and dog behavior:

Dodman, Nicholas H. *Dogs Behaving Badly: An A–Z Guide to Understanding and Curing Behavioral Problems in Dogs.* Bantam Doubleday Dell Publishers, 1999.

Lachman, Larry. *Dogs on the Couch: Behavior Therapy for Training and Caring for Your Dog.* Overlook Press, 1999.

Masson, Jeffrey Moussaieff. *Dogs Never Lie About Love: Reflections on the Emotional World of Dogs*. Random House, 1998.

O'Brien, Jacqui. *Train Your Dog*. Barron's Educational Series, Inc., 1999.

Owens, Paul, and Norma Eckroate. *The Dog Whisperer: A Compassionate, Nonviolent Approach to Dog Training*. Adams Media Corporation, 1999.

Shojai, Amy. *Competability: A Practical Guide to Building a Peaceable Kingdom Between Cats and Dogs*. Three Rivers Press, 1998.

To teach children pet safety, try the video *Dogs, Cats and Kids*. Pet Partnerships, P.O. Box 11331, Chicago, IL 60611-0331, 1-800-784-0979.

To find a certified applied animal behaviorist, visit the Animal Behavior Society's web page at *www.cisab.indiana.edu/ABS/Applied/index.html* for the most up-to-date listing. You can also contact the Association of Pet Dog Trainers (APDT) at 1-800-PET-DOGS. This is a national registry of qualified people from across the United States.

For more information about clicker training, see these resources:

Spector, Morgan. *Clicker Training for Obedience Competition: Getting Top Performance—Positively!* Sunshine Books, 1998.

Check out these other commercial web sites on clicker training:

www.ClickerTrain.com/

www.clickandtreat.com/

Clicker training material also can be ordered on-line from *www.amazon.com/*.

The Clicker Journal offers tips, techniques, anecdotes, and analysis for and by people who are experimenting with clicker training. The *Journal* includes a wide variety of applications. To subscribe, write to *The Clicker Journal*, 20146 Gleedsville Road, Leesburg, VA 22075. Subscriptions are $18 per year.

Seasonal Tips

Included in this chapter are survival tips that follow your dog through the seasons of the year and the seasons of his life. Included are tips for battling the heat and cold, helping your dog if he has access to the outdoors, and traveling with your dog.

Don't Give Me Any Static

Have you ever stooped to touch your dog and seen a spark fly or felt a jolt as your fingers made contact with his hair? During the winter, when the air inside your home is dry, you may experience a slight charge from the buildup of static electricity when you pet your dog. Although the charge is enough to give you and your dog a shock, it's not enough to cause damage to you or your animal companion. If static electricity is giving you static, you can eliminate it with some of these ideas.

• You can help eliminate static buildup on your dog by using cleansing wipes that add moisture to his coat.

• To help control static when you touch your dog, use an anti-static product in the clothes dryer when you dry your clothes.

• Try a pet moisturizing spray to help eliminate dry skin as a way to control static buildup.

• Use a humidifier to add moisture to the air and prevent the buildup of static electricity.

- Place basins of water throughout the house to add moisture to the air if you don't have a humidifier.

- Use an antistatic product on your carpet. Spray it on but be sure to allow it to dry before letting your pooch walk on it.

- Wipe your dog's hair with an antistatic dryer sheet.

Gardening with Pets in Mind

Your plants, whether indoors or out, may have a special appeal to your dog. Your dog may enjoy digging up your geraniums or depositing wastes on your watermelons. Or, he may find it fun to dig the dirt from your houseplants and then deposit it on the floor for later use. If you notice dogs that are not your own entering your yard or digging in your garden, try to find out whose they are and discuss with the owners about keeping them indoors or leashed. Many communities have leash laws, so you may have legal muscle to back up your friendly discussions. If the dogs don't belong to anyone, refer to the section in this chapter on rescuing free-roaming dogs (page 83). To keep your dog from starting his own landscaping business, try some of these tips for turning your four-legged dirt devil into a lawn lover.

- Check at farm or garden stores for chemical products developed to repel animals from choosing your garden as a favorite place to dig or deposit wastes. Such products come in granular forms that last up to three months outside. The odor is designed to stop animals from leaving their droppings around your home.

- Sprinkle alum powder around bushes or objects in your garden your dog likes to dig up.

• To keep both cats and dogs from digging in your outdoor garden, sprinkle the garden with moth crystals. If you have kids, cover the moth crystals with dirt.

• If your dog likes to dig in a certain spot, try placing upside-down mousetraps that will startle him if he disturbs them.

• If your gardens are of the container variety or consist entirely of indoor plants, prevent your dog from digging in the potted soil by inserting pine or other evergreen cones in the dirt. Or, place aluminum foil over the pot.

• Bury a cotton ball dipped in oil of cloves just below the surface of the soil in your flowerpots. Be sure it is just barely covered by the soil.

• If you use a chemical lawn treatment, insecticide, or fertilizer, make sure your dog stays off the lawn for the specified amount of time (usually 24 hours), depending on the product you use. When walking your dog, be on the lookout for signs placed in yards by lawn treatment companies alerting you to the presence of chemicals in the grass and keep your dog off those areas until the signs are removed.

• If you've used a lawn flea treatment, keep your dog off the lawn until it is safe. Read the product label directions to determine how long your dog should keep off the grass.

• The best way to keep a dog from digging in your garden and flower beds is to surround the gardens and beds with fencing or chicken wire that is high enough to prevent them from jumping over and inserted about 1 foot (30 cm) under the ground to prevent them from digging under them.

• As a last resort, and if surrounding your garden with a real fence is impossible, try an invisible fencing system that creates a barrier that your dog won't jump over or dig under. The invisible fencing system is customized to your dog, home, and property (see page 82).

- If your dog digs out of boredom, play with him more often and allow him to participate in family events or trips.

- If your dog digs holes to escape his fenced-in area, he could benefit from walks around the neighborhood where he will increase his social contacts among the resident animals.

- If your dog likes to dig in the garden, offer him his own space to dig, instead of trying to stop him. Put his toys, some treats, and a water bowl in the area.

Hot Dogs

The dog days of summer have special meaning for your dog. Warm weather brings a host of problems for dogs, whose furry coats hold the heat. Left outside in the sun, dogs can suffer heat exhaustion or heatstroke. Because dogs have no sweat glands distributed throughout their bodies, they are more susceptible to heat-related discomforts and must rely on panting or sweating via their footpads as a self-defense mechanism to deal with the heat and humidity. Like you, your dog will appreciate some help battling hot or humid weather.

- Air conditioning is the best way to help your dog stay cool in the warm weather, but if you don't have that luxury, place fans in places where your dog likes to sleep. Window fans set on exhaust will help circulate the air inside your home and keep your dog from heating up.

- Allow your dog access to cooler rooms of the house, such as the basement, the garage, or a screened porch where there's a breeze.

- Place some old pillowcases in a plastic bag and put them in the freezer. Take one out on really hot days for your dog to sleep on.

- Keep an ice pack handy. On hot days, place it under your dog's bedding to cool your pooch off as he snoozes.

- Keep your dog's water dish filled with fresh, cool water. Place ice cubes in the water during the hottest periods of the day.

- During extremely hot weather, keep heavy exercise to a minimum and play with your dog during the cooler parts of the day.

- Older and overweight dogs are more at risk from the heat, so be more sensitive to them in warm weather.

- To prevent heat exhaustion and possibly death *never* leave your dog in a closed car in the summer heat.

- To help your dog stay cool outside, purchase a Canine Cooler Thermoregulating Pet Bed that absorbs heat and disperses it, making him always feel cool.

- Attach a water bottle like those used in rabbit hutches to a wire kennel for your dog to drink from.

- Attach a "licker" to an outdoor faucet or hose in your dog's run. When he's thirsty, he licks the device to get fresh water. The licker can be attached to a hose and extended into your dog's run.

- An alternative way to allow your pooch to have water when he is outside is to pound a stake in the ground in his outdoor area. Place an angel food or bundt cake pan with an opening in the center over the stake to keep your dog from tipping over the pan. Fill the pan with water.

- Buy a child's swimming pool and fill it with water for your dog to get into.

- Place wet towels in your dog's outdoor run or doghouse to help him stay cool.

- If your dog has an outdoor doghouse, cover the floor with cedar shavings to help control parasites and retain the moisture in his skin.

- If your dog stays outside in a doghouse, make certain the house is placed in the shade. A doghouse heated by the summer sun can be almost as deadly as a closed automobile.

- If you live in a warm climate, paint your doghouse white. This reflects light rather than absorbs it; a white doghouse will stay cooler than one that is dark in color.

Old Man Winter

Snowflakes that fall on your nose and eyelashes may be a few of Julie Andrews' favorite things, but your dog may think other-wise. Cold, frigid weather presents the same problems for pets as it does for humans. If your dog is uncomfortable in the cold, expect him to shiver or hold up his paws as he walks. Left outside

HOW-TO: Recognize Heat Stress

Heat-related problems in dogs include heat exhaustion (from prolonged exposure to intense heat) or heatstroke (from exposure to high temperatures and humidity). Dogs suffering from heat stresses may suffer cellular breakdown, brain damage, and heart failure resulting in death. If your dog is elderly, over-weight, suffers from cardiovascular or respiratory problems, or is one of the short-nosed breeds, he could be more susceptible to heat-related stresses. If your dog is left in the sun, has exercised strenuously on a hot day, or is left in a closed car in warm weather, the symptoms listed below could signal danger.

- *Anxious expression*
- *Dazed or unconscious state*
- *Heavy panting*
- *High fever (above 104°F [40°C])*
- *Lethargy, fatigue*
- *Pawing at doors or kennel openings*
- *Salivating*
- *Staggering*
- *Vomiting, diarrhea*
- *Warm, dry skin*
- *Weakness*

If you suspect your dog is suffering from heat exhaustion or heatstroke, reduce his temperature by immersing him in a tub or container of tepid water or water him down with a hose or wet towels. Don't use ice or ice water because when your dog is overheated, the extremely cold temperature of the ice could cause shock. Take your dog to a veterinarian immediately.

for extended periods of time, your dog can experience frostbite or hypothermia. Look for discoloring of the skin, especially on the ear tips and other extremities. If you find any signs, contact your veterinarian. Salt or other ice-melting chemicals as well as antifreeze can be extremely hazardous and life-threatening for the dog that ingests them. Road salt also can cause sores if it becomes lodged between your dog's footpads. Dogs at risk from the cold and winter-related hazards, whether they live indoors or out, need special care.

• Place a flannel sheet over your dog's bed for extra warmth.

• To keep warm, your dog may like to sleep on floor heating vents that can catch the identification tags attached to his collar. If your dog likes to snooze over a floor vent, put his tags in a Pet Pocket (see Resources in the chapter on safety, page 35), which attaches to his collar.

• In cold weather, your dog will need more energy to fight the cold in the form of extra calories, so don't be afraid to offer him additional food in the winter.

• Be sure to wipe off your dog's paws when he comes in from the outside to prevent salt and other chemicals from sticking to his feet.

• Keep antifreeze out of your dog's reach, and be sure to clean up any that may have spilled in the garage or driveway.

• If your dog is accustomed to living the good life indoors, don't allow him to stay outside for extended periods of time in cold weather.

• Make sure your dog has a warm, draft-free place to sleep. Since warm air rises, offering him a bed off the floor will add extra warmth and comfort for winter dreaming.

• Don't allow your dog to be off leash in a snowstorm or ice storm. If he gets lost, he will not be able to use his sense of smell to find his way home.

• If your dog is shorthaired, elderly, or sensitive to the cold, even for short walks, consider purchasing a sweater for him to wear in cold weather.

Outdoor Access

Nothing beats a walk in the fresh air and sunshine for a dog (and owner!). Going for a walk gives your pooch a chance to savor the smells of the great outdoors. Dogs are social creatures and walking provides them with opportunities to meet other people and other dogs. If you can't always walk your dog, allowing him outside offers him a way to have some fun and take part in additional activities during the day. Outdoor access can be safe if your dog goes from the house into an enclosure. Dogs should not be

HOW-TO: Cold-Proof Your Dog's Outdoor Kennel

If your dog stays in an outdoor kennel, provide a warm, draft-free doghouse that is insulated against the cold.

1. *The doghouse should be no more than 12 inches (30 cm) longer or 3 inches (7.6 cm) higher than the dog because a dog's body heat cannot raise the environmental temperature in a doghouse that is too large.*
2. *Be sure your dog's house has a floor and raise it off the ground to keep it and your dog from becoming soaked by rain or snow.*
3. *If you are constructing a doghouse yourself, place the entrance off center so that your dog can sleep away from drafts.*
4. *Put straw inside the doghouse for warmth and cover the doghouse door with a flap or piece of carpet to shelter your dog from the wind.*
4. *Place the doghouse so it is facing south for added warmth.*
5. *When the temperature drops below freezing, give your dog a heated water bowl so he has continual access to water.*
6. *Do not use metal food bowls because your dog's tongue may stick to them in freezing weather.*

allowed to roam freely outside for their own protection and the protection of neighbors and property. If you allow your dog access to a fenced-in yard or enclosure, follow some of these suggestions to make life easier for you and him.

• If you would like your dog to have unrestricted access to your yard, enclose it to prevent him from escaping or other animals from entering.

• If you don't want to construct a fence around your yard, investigate invisible fencing systems that prevent your dog from leaving the yard by a radio signal. With these systems your dog wears a collar that emits a small electronic charge when he gets to the fence boundary. *Caution: Although invisible fencing may prevent your dog from leaving your yard, it does not protect him from other animals or strangers entering your yard. Electronic fences should be advertised at the street level to let people walking dogs on leashes know that the dog in your yard will not chase after them. If you have an aggressive dog, don't rely on an invisible fence to retain him.*

• Investigate prefab or standardized enclosures or pens. Check the classifieds in the major dog magazines or catalogs or on-line stores listed in the last chapter.

• Place a grass mat inside your dog's pet door to prevent him from tracking mud inside the house.

• A plastic carpet runner at the door will protect carpeting from muddy pet footprints.

• Keep a supply of towels handy when bringing your dog inside from a walk in rain or snow.

• If your dog goes into an outdoor enclosure at will, keep him confined to the room into which the pet door opens until you have an opportunity to wash his feet and check for fleas and ticks. For example, if your pet door is in the laundry room, keep the laundry room door closed until you make your dog house-ready.

- If you must walk your dog in the rain, an automatically opening umbrella allows you to keep one hand on his leash while the other holds the umbrella.

- Rubber boots will protect your dog's feet when he walks outside; they can be removed easily upon entering your house.

- Choke collars or spiked collars pose a special hazard to dogs that wear them when being tied outside. To prevent possible choking, never allow your dog to be tied outside with a choke or spiked collar. They are only to be used when walking or conducting training sessions.

Rescuing Free-Roaming Dogs

If a dog begins hanging around your house, and you cannot find his owner, chances are the animal is a stray. The life of a stray dog is not a pleasant one. Strays are at risk from other animals, cars, uncaring or abusive humans, contagious diseases, and anything that can cause them pain and suffering and bring their lives to an untimely end. By rescuing a stray, you will be saving a life and helping reduce animal overpopulation. Even if you take the dog to a shelter, you will give him some hope of finding a home.

Traveling with Your Dog

In this time of change, mobility is the operative word for the modern world. On some occasions, our travels are just around the corner, and on others, our trips are across town or across the country. Whether we are moving, vacationing, or simply taking a pet to the veterinarian, traveling with our pets is certain to occur sooner or later.

By land

Sharing the company of your favorite canine companion on the road can add an extra measure of pleasure to your excursions. Perhaps you are moving and plan to take your dog in the car with you. Before you hit the road, some pre-trip planning is in order. Follow these suggestions for making a car trip more enjoyable for both you and your dog.

• Before committing to taking your dog along with you on a vacation, think about whether he will enjoy the trip. Dogs seem to like

HOW-TO: Trap a Free-Roaming Domestic Dog

*Occasionally, you may find a dog that comes willingly to you and eagerly accepts an invitation into your home. However, not all stray animals go eagerly to their human saviors, so arming yourself with some ingenuity and information may be the only way to convince a stray that life with you will be better than life on the streets. If you decide to pursue capturing that stray dog, be careful and don't risk being injured yourself. Stray or injured animals may be stressed and frightened, and your attempt to help may cause them to react defensively or behave unpredictably. **Caution: If you have other pets, be sure to isolate the stray until you can have the new animal examined by a veterinarian and tested for parasites and contagious diseases.***

Dogs and dog ownership are often governed by the laws of the municipalities in which they live or are found. If you find a free-roaming dog, follow these guidelines before you decide to make the dog your own.

1. When you see a free-roaming dog, contact your local police, humane organization, or animal control authorities to determine what procedures, if any, you are required to follow for the dog's capture. The solution may be as simple as providing the exact location where you saw the dog so that someone can come and catch him.

2. If you have determined that you can catch the dog yourself, speak gently to him and offer some food.

3. If the dog is wearing a collar with identification tags, contact the owner. The owner may be unaware that the dog is missing. If the dog is not wearing tags, notify your local animal control authorities. If you have caught the dog, you may be obligated to turn him over and wait for a specified period of time in case the owner is attempting to find him.

4. If the dog is injured, take him to a veterinarian or emergency veterinary clinic. Be prepared to pay the fees for the dog's treatment, however.

5. If you would like to keep the dog, let the animal control authorities know that you will provide a home if the owner is not found.

to ride in cars or trucks, but some panicky pooches may do better if left at home. Your dog may bark, cry, or whine during the entire trip, making you as miserable as he is. If you are planning a vacation and you think your dog might prefer to stay home, consider leaving your unhappy camper in the care of a professional pet-sitter or someone else you trust.

• New experiences, smells, locations, and people can cause stress to even the most intrepid dog traveler. If your dog experiences stress or motion sickness, he might develop diarrhea, vomit, pant excessively, or drool. To minimize stress, keep everything as normal as possible. On the trip, give your dog the same food he is accustomed to eating and take along a supply of his usual water.

• Make certain that your dog's vaccinations and shots are up to date and carry vaccination certificates and veterinary information with you. If you cross an international border, board your dog during the trip, or seek veterinary medical help, you may be required to show proof of vaccinations. Take along your veterinarian's phone number and any medications your dog might need.

• Take a care pack that includes your dog's regular food, a food bowl and heavy water dish that won't tip over, a supply of water, an emergency kit, extra blankets, leashes, some toys, grooming tools, and paper towels. If you are traveling in warm weather, take an ice pack to place in your dog's carrier or next to him on the car seat. For a nontipping dish, check your local automotive supply store for large cup holders with sandbag bottoms or purchase a nonspill pet dish designed for that purpose.

• Don't feed your dog for about three hours before beginning your trip. If you like, offer him a snack while riding, but don't provide dinner until you arrive at your destination.

- Make certain your dog is wearing a collar with identification tags. If he escapes without ID tags, you may never find him again. Take along a photo of your dog in case you do get separated.

- If your dog suffers from carsickness, discuss medication options with your veterinarian.

- Don't leave your dog in a parked automobile during the day in warm months. The inside of the vehicle can reach 120°F (49°C) or more very quickly. Even venting the window is not enough to provide circulating air, and your dog could suffocate and die. If you must make a rest stop, make it brief or take your dog with you. Park in the shade.

- If you don't have air conditioning in your vehicle, travel at night or during cooler times of the day.

- Keep your dog in a carrier or crate at all times and secure the carrier with a seat belt or other device; if you roll down the window, your dog could escape.

- Make frequent rest stops so your dog can relieve himself or have a drink of water.

- If your trip requires overnight accommodations, know ahead of time which hotels accept pets. Make reservations and let them know you will be bringing an animal. If you are camping, make certain the campsite or RV park allows pets.

- Two of the most hazardous ways to travel with a dog are to allow the dog to hang out the window or to allow him to ride in the back of a pickup truck. To prevent your dog from leaping out of the vehicle window or injuring himself if you must come to a sudden stop, keep your dog inside your car or truck and crated or leashed while traveling. If you put your dog's crate in the back of a pickup truck, clamp the crate to the truck bed for safety.

• Before you and your dog exit your vehicle, leash your dog. During nighttime travel, wear reflective clothing and put a reflective collar on your dog before going for a stroll along the highway.

By air

Sometimes flying is the best way to travel, and that may involve taking your dog on board an airplane or shipping him ahead. Although thousands of pets are transported by air every year, when the occasional one succumbs to an airline mishap during transport, it makes headlines. Horror stories abound about pets shipped in too-hot or too-cold cargo containers, who, as a result, have either suffocated or frozen to death. But airline awareness about travel for pets has improved in recent years. You can help minimize risks to your dog by following these guidelines.

• Contact the airline in advance to determine their pet regulations. Try to book a direct flight or one with a minimum number of stops. Travel on the same flight as your dog and ask to see him being loaded into the cargo hold. If possible, fly during the cool parts of the day in warm weather and warm parts of the day in cool weather.

• Investigate an airline's pet transport policies and procedures before buying your dog a ticket. Find out what the accommodations are like. Is the cargo hold climate controlled? How long will your dog have to wait before he is brought off the plane at its destination? What other types of cargo will be shipped on your flight? Will someone hand-deliver your dog, or will he be whisked into the airport along with the luggage?

• If you have a small dog, you may be able to take the animal on board with you as long as he is in a carrier that fits under the seat in front of you. Contact the airlines to determine if this method of transport is allowed and for the accepted crate size.

• The Humane Society of the United States recommends not shipping short-nosed dogs, such as Pekingese, Chows, or Pugs, or cats in airplane cargo holds. Because of their shortened nasal passages, these breeds are more vulnerable to oxygen deprivation and heatstroke.

• If your dog is to be shipped in the cargo hold, purchase a sturdy, United States Department of Agriculture–approved carrier or shipping crate that is large enough for him to stand up and move around in. It should have adequate ventilation, and the words "Live Animals" should appear on the front top of the crate.

HOW-TO: Find a Pet-sitter

If you would prefer to leave Fido in the comfort of his own home while you are on vacation or a business trip, hire a professional pet-sitter to care for your dog while you are away. Using a professional pet-sitter will eliminate any potential stress caused by being transported and reduce the health risk of being around strange animals. A pet-sitter will feed, water, and play with your dog, walk him, water your plants, bring in the newspaper and mail, turn lights on and off, feed the fish if you have any, as well as help give your home a lived-in look while you're not there. Follow these steps to find a pet-sitter.

1. *Begin the process of finding a pet-sitter well in advance of your trip. Pet-sitters, like boarding kennels, are booked early, especially over the holidays or during prime vacation time.*
2. *Ask your veterinarian or pet-owning friends for a referral. Finding a sitter who is trustworthy and has a good reputation is important for your peace of mind.*
3. *If you cannot get a referral, check the Yellow Pages of your telephone directory under "Pet-sitters." Call several and set up appointments to interview them. As an alternative, call the locator lines of the two major professional pet-sitting organizations for a list of member pet-sitters in your area.*
4. *When you call a pet-sitter, ask if he or she is bonded and insured and can supply you with references. Ask how long he or she has been in business and what experience with animals the person has beyond pet-sitting.*
5. *Set up a meeting with the pet-sitter so that you and your pet can meet him or her. The sitter should be interested in your animal and attempt to establish a rapport during the first meeting. Getting to know the pet sometimes takes a while if the pet is shy, but the sitter should make the effort.*
6. *Expect the sitter to ask you questions about your dog's care, including feeding, walking, cleaning up, disposing of doggie wastes, recycling pet food cans, and games your dog likes to play.*

Put some comfortable blankets or bedding on the bottom of the crate. Close the crate securely but don't lock it in case airport personnel must open it in an emergency.

• Fit your dog with ID tags that have your name, address, and phone number as well as the address and phone number of your destination. Carry a photo of your dog in case he is lost.

• Know what, if any, quarantine requirements might be in effect at your travel destination. The state of Hawaii requires that incoming pets be quarantined for four months and the countries comprising Great Britain have a six-month quarantine. If you're planning a

7. When you decide on a sitter, expect to sign a contract covering the dates of care, cost, and liabilities. Some sitters, like housekeepers, require payment up front, so don't be put off by a sitter asking for payment in advance. When you sign the contract, you will need to give the sitter the key. Decide at that time if you want the sitter to leave the key in your home on the last visit or keep the key until you return. If no one else has a key to your home, it may be safer for your dog if you allow the sitter to hang onto the key until you've returned from your trip.

8. Be sure to let the sitter know of any illnesses or idiosyncracies that your dog has so that the sitter is not surprised if he behaves in a particular way. For example, does your dog get fatigued easily, or does he hide from strangers?

9. If your dog eats little while you are gone, let the sitter know and offer suggestions of what to do if he decides to go on a hunger strike. If you free-feed your dog, ask the sitter to measure each meal to determine if he is eating it.

10. Provide the sitter with important information such as the phone number of where you will be, anyone locally to notify in an emergency, and the name and number of your veterinarian.

11. Inform your veterinarian that you will be away. Have your veterinarian keep a letter on file from you that says you are going away and names the pet-sitter and service as your dog's temporary guardian. If there is a problem, the sitter will have the authority to bring him in and you will be responsible for any fees.

12. The sitter should give you a business card to take with you so that you can call the sitter if you need to for any reason. If your return is going to be delayed, contact the sitter to take care of your dog for the additional time.

13. Contact the sitter when you return to let her or him know you are back.

two-week jaunt to either of these locations or other ones that will force your dog to spend his time there in a cage to see what diseases might develop, don't bother taking him along.

• Make certain your dog is up to date on vaccinations. Take the necessary certificates with you.

• Don't feed your dog or give him water less than four hours before the flight. Do not tranquilize your dog before flying.

• Once at your destination, have your dog checked by a veterinarian to make certain he has arrived in good health and has withstood the stress of the trip.

Waging War on Allergies (Your Own)

Does the presence of your dog cause you to sneeze unmercifully? Do your eyes fill with tears of misery instead of tears of joy when your canine companion wants to be close? Many of us who love animals find that we can't even pet them without the ahhs becoming the ahh-choos! Miserable allergies prevent us from sharing our lives with the four-legged friends we adore. Pet allergies can cause watery eyes, nasal congestion, runny nose, sneezing, scratchy, sore throat, coughing, wheezing, and even hives. Cats and dogs are the two most common animals to produce allergic reactions in people. The primary cause of allergic reactions to dogs is the dander, or dead skin scales that they shed into the environment, but saliva or urine may also cause a person to experience allergic responses. Breeds of dogs whose skin sheds more rapidly, such as Cocker and Springer Spaniels, Shar-Peis, Basset Hounds, German Shepherd Dogs, Irish Setters, Doberman Pinschers, Dachshunds, and Afghan Hounds, are more likely to cause allergic reactions. Allergies may not develop immediately when a person adopts a pet, but may take several years to surface as the allergens build up in the home. To keep you responding to your dog instead of reacting to him, try some of these suggestions.

- Restrict the areas in your home to which your dog has access.

- Wash your bedding weekly.

- Make sure you have your allergy shots and take any medication your doctor advises.

- Purchase a high-efficiency particulate air (HEPA) filter to remove allergens from your home.

- Eliminate carpets, draperies, and stuffed furniture from the bedroom to keep your pillows, mattress, and bedding allergen free. Treat carpet and upholstered furniture in other rooms with an anti-allergen dust spray.

- Use allergen-proof vacuum cleaner bags.

Resources

For more information about airplane travel regulations, contact the United States Department of Agriculture's Animal and Plant Health Inspection Service automated information line at 800-545-USDA (8732) and follow the instructions.

Try one of these books to find pet-friendly boarding or things to do with your pet while on the road:

Ludwig, Gerd. *Fun and Games with Your Dog.* Barron's Educational Series, Inc., 1996.

Smith, Cheryl. *On the Trail with Your Canine Companion: Getting the Most out of Hiking and Camping with Your Dog.* Howell Book House, 1996.

Walters, Heather MacLean. *Take Your Pet Too!: Fun Things to Do!* M.C.E., 1997.

Weekes, Greg. *Traveling with Your Pet 1999: The AAA Guide to More Than 10,000 Pet-Friendly, AAA Rated Lodgings Across the United States and Canada.* American Automobile Association, 1999.

Or, if you want to hit the road with Rover, check out one of the titles from the *Dog Lover Series* that includes *The Atlanta Dog Lover's Companion, The Boston Dog Lover's Companion, The Florida Dog Lover's Companion,* and more, from Foghorn Press.

Writer Eileen Barish takes you and your dog traveling all over the United States with the *Vacationing with Your Pet Series* that includes titles such as *Doin' Arizona with Your Pooch,* and *Doin' Texas with Your Pooch,* all from Pet Friendly Productions.

For locations of pet-sitters near you, contact these organizations:

Pet Sitters International locator line: 1-800-268-SITS.

National Association of Professional Pet Sitters locator line: 1-800-296-PETS.

Helpful Hints for Dogs with Disabilities

Have you ever seen a three-legged dog run and jump for a Frisbee? A deaf dog come for his dinner when the electric can opener is turned on? To us, a dog that has lost limbs or the use of some of his senses may seem incapable of enjoying life, but appearances may be deceiving. Just because your dog is growing older, has become blind or hard of hearing, lost the use of his legs, or experienced some other debilitating illness or injury, don't assume that the animal cannot live a normal life or that his behavior will change for the worse. When it comes to dealing with disabilities, animals have the advantage; they don't sit around and pine about what they can no longer do. Unless they are so ill or injured that they cannot function at all, the disabled dog will adjust to his limitations.

Aging Dogs

Your dog may live between ten and fifteen years depending in part on the breed, with an average of twelve years longevity. Aging is a natural process and results in changes in your dog's metabolism, hormone balance, and sensory perception. A dog is considered to be a senior at the age of seven or eight. Your aging dog will sleep more and experience degeneration of his body systems and internal organs. Expect him, as he gets older, to have less tolerance of extremes in heat or cold, decreased immunity to disease and infection, and a decline in his metabolism. Older dogs may lose their vision and hearing. Because the older dog is generally less active, he requires fewer calories. If you have children in the house, make certain that they understand that your family dog is elderly and requires more careful and sensitive handling.

• As your dog grows older, have your veterinarian run appropriate tests to detect any illness or degenerative condition early so he can be treated. Pay attention to any changes in your dog's habits, behavior, or appearance and report them to your veterinarian.

• Learn the symptoms of some of the more common problems that afflict the older dog, such as diabetes, kidney and thyroid problems, and heart conditions. If you notice any symptoms, contact your veterinarian right away.

• Discuss with your veterinarian feeding your geriatric dog a diet formulated specifically for the needs of older animals.

• As your dog ages, look for signs of dental problems. Clean your dog's teeth regularly and have your veterinarian professionally clean them when necessary.

• Pets become more creatures of habit as they age. If you are planning any environmental changes, do so gradually and pay special attention to your dog's needs to minimize any stress he experiences.

• When you groom your geriatric dog, look for lumps and bumps under the skin and report them to your veterinarian.

• Engage your older dog in moderate play to promote muscle tone, increase circulation, and aid digestion.

• Have your dog leashed when he is outside to keep him safe and help him live longer.

Arthritis or Stiffness

As dogs age, their joints can stiffen and arthritis can set in. There is no cure for arthritis, but some of these suggestions may help to alleviate your dog's arthritic pain and make performing everyday functions a lot easier.

• Keep your dog's weight at a normal level—added weight will put more stress on bones, joints, and muscles.

• Don't give aspirin to your dog unless advised to do so by your veterinarian—aspirin can be extremely toxic.

• Make a set of steps or use footstools to help your dog reach his destination, such as his favorite sleeping chair. If the steps are wooden, tack carpeting to them to prevent him from slipping.

• To help a dog maneuver up the steps or climb to a favorite spot, make a carpet-covered ramp. If you build an outdoor ramp, use outdoor-grade plywood covered with outdoor carpeting to keep the footing secure. Carpet scraps and squares can be purchased at carpet outlets.

• Give your dog elevated food and water bowls to keep him from having to bend over to eat. The elevated bowl will help relieve arthritic pain and aid digestion.

• As an alternative, place your dog's food bowls in a stacking in/out tray designed for the office to raise them off the floor. The modular design will help you find the perfect height for your pet.

Blindness or Vision Problems

As with most other physical limitations, your dog will adapt to loss of sight and learn to function by using his other senses. Occasionally, the loss occurs slowly as the dog ages rather than suddenly, giving him more time to adjust. You can help by following some of these suggestions.

• Don't lift a blind dog. Because blind dogs use spatial relationships to find their way around, lifting them causes disorientation and confusion when they are placed back down on the floor.

• Keep objects and furniture in the same spots around the house because blind dogs use their memory and familiarity with their surroundings to find their way around. Rearranging the furniture confuses the blind pet and adds hazards to its environment.

• If your house is large, try restricting your blind dog to a small area of it so that he can learn his way around more quickly and easily. Gradually allow him access to the rest of the house.

• If your dog has cataracts or low vision, keep a light turned on at night to help him see.

• If your dog's vision problems are due to cataracts, they can be removed surgically. Discuss options with your veterinarian.

• Construct a collar-mounted "walking cane" for your blind dog that curves forward and to the side to warn him of an impending object.

• To help your dog become accustomed to steps or objects on his walk, choose a command, such as "*Wait*," and use it when you and your dog approach a step. Stop and allow your dog to put his nose down to determine the source of the problem.

• If you allow your blind dog to go outside into your yard, fence your yard or construct a smaller enclosure so he can have safe access to the outdoors. Keep objects in your yard in the same places to prevent your dog from bumping into them.

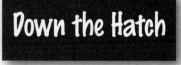

Down the Hatch

Your dog's desire for food is determined as much by his sense of smell as it is by his sense of taste. If the food doesn't smell good, your dog won't eat it, no matter how much you think he should. When your dog comes down with a cold or flu that affects his ability to smell his dinner, his appetite may not be what it normally is, and if your dog is suffering from an illness, he may not want to eat. When your dog is sick is the time he most needs nourishment, however, and at those times, you may have to offer a helping hand to encourage him to devour dinner.

• Pour some of the drippings from your roast beef over his dry food to make it more appealing.

• Offer him some wet food in a lamb variety to encourage him to eat.

• When you open a bag of dry food, place a few beef jerky strips in the bag. The aroma from the jerky will seep into the food and make it more appealing to your dog.

Hearing Problems

Deafness or hearing loss in dogs may be due to genetic factors or the result of disease, injury, drug toxicity, or old age. Deaf dogs can function just as normally as those that can hear as long as you take a few precautions. Because your dog has no sense of hearing, he will rely on his other senses to take over. To help your deaf dog manage, try some of these suggestions.

• Dogs shouldn't run loose, but not allowing a dog free run is especially important when he can't hear the threat of danger such as oncoming traffic. As a safety precaution, don't allow deaf dogs unrestricted access to the outdoors.

- Because a deaf dog can't hear you approach, make certain he sees you before you touch him. Touching a deaf dog before he is aware of your presence may cause him to react defensively.

- Use visual clues to get your deaf dog's attention. Hand signals call him to your side when the sound of your voice won't.

- Try tapping on the floor with your fingers. The tapping will make slight vibrations that will get your deaf dog's attention.

- Instead of clicker training, use a flashlight flicked on and off to obedience-train your dog, or thumbs up and thumbs down signals.

HOW-TO: Provide Quality Home Care for the Sick Dog

When your dog is sick, caring for him in the comfort of his own home whenever possible will help reduce stress and hasten recovery. If you would like to care for your dog at home rather than have him hospitalized, discuss the options with your veterinarian. Make certain you know what is involved and that you can provide whatever care is necessary.

1. *Discuss with your veterinarian any at-home treatment that must be administered to your dog, including medication, diet, exercise, or checkups following the illness or surgery.*
2. *If appropriate, set up a sick room for your dog with his bed, food, and water. If you detect that your dog would rather be with the members of the family, allow him that option. A sick room environment is only beneficial to a dog if he wants to be alone during recovery.*
3. *If you must administer medication, prepare a schedule for doing so or put the pill times on your daily planner or calendar.*
4. *Make sure your dog's bed is in a draft-free location. For extra warmth, add a blanket or flannel sheet or use a hot water bottle wrapped in a towel or heating pad. A heat lamp also may be used as an extra source of heat but be sure to keep it high above your dog's bed to prevent accidental burning.*
5. *Keep your recovering dog eating. Nourishment will speed the process. If your dog doesn't want to eat, follow some of the suggestions on page 97.*
6. *If your dog can't keep himself clean, wipe him off with a sponge or cloth dampened with warm water. Dry him as soon as you are finished with the sponge bath. While your dog is ill, do not bathe him in water.*
7. *Provide plenty of fresh water for your convalescing dog. There are now systems available that circulate, filter, and aerate the water and are designed to give your dog a constant supply of good-quality water as well as promote urinary tract health.*

• Some dogs that cannot hear most sounds do pick up on high-pitched noises such as those emitted by dog whistles. Try using a dog whistle to call your deaf dog.

• To call your deaf dog to dinner or get his attention, flick lights on and off.

• Deaf dogs that are a part of a multi-pet family often take their clues from the actions of other pets in the household. Your deaf dog may like to have a companion to help him along.

• Discuss with your veterinarian the option of obtaining a hearing aid for your dog. Hearing aids are not appropriate for all animals suffering hearing loss, but your dog may be a candidate if he has some hearing left.

Incontinence

Incontinence happens, to paraphrase the popular bumper sticker, and it may occur temporarily due to a bladder infection or permanently due to other illnesses or physical conditions. Before following any suggestion to deal with the incontinence, have your dog examined by a veterinarian to determine the source of the problem. If the incontinence is caused by an infection, it can be treated with antibiotics.

• Place pet pads that are plastic on one side and quilted on the other to absorb moisture or newspapers around the house so that your dog can get to them easily.

• Investigate using pet diapers on your incontinent dog. Often, they are used for females in heat who may dribble urine.

• If your dog's incontinence was temporary due to a bladder infection, you may have to retrain him to urinate outside once the infection has cleared. Clean any urine spots with a good odor neutralizer so that your dog won't return to them the next time he must potty.

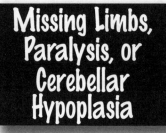

Missing Limbs, Paralysis, or Cerebellar Hypoplasia

Dogs with missing or unusable limbs can adapt quite well to their situation, especially if they are given a little help from their owners. If your dog has lost a limb or the use of one or both, try some of these suggestions to help him get a leg up on his condition.

• Wheelchairs are available for pets with missing hind limbs, back problems, arthritis, paralysis, or other maladies. The K-9 Cart or a product called Doggon' Wheels keeps your dog's hind legs off the ground so they bear no weight while he propels himself using his front legs.

• Carpeted ramps throughout the house will help a dog with ambulatory difficulties to get up on furniture or move to any location that involves steps.

• Put your dog's bed on the floor in a draft-free spot to keep him from having to climb into bed. If your dog wants to sleep with you, provide carpeted climbing ramps.

• Use piles of pillows to ease your handicapped dog's transition to a higher location. The pillows will help him pull himself up and provide cushioning if he should fall.

Pill Popping Time

Getting the pill into your dog can be frustrating when he has other ideas about what he wants to put into his mouth. If your dog gives you flak at pill popping time, try some of these tricks to maneuver the medicine into his mouth.

• Your veterinarian may be able to give you medicine for your dog in a variety of forms, so if you think it will be easier to administer liquid medicine, for example, ask if it comes in liquid form. Capsules seem to be the most difficult form of medicine to administer, so inquire whether the capsule contents can be removed and mixed with food.

- To administer liquid medicine, use a dosing syringe and quickly squirt the medicine into your dog's mouth.

- A pill gun is a quick and effective way to give your dog a pill. They are available from veterinarians.

- Crush the pills and mix with water. Give them to your dog in a syringe.

- If the medication is a pill, roll a piece of cream cheese around it like a tiny meatball and watch your dog eat it without hassle.

- To make sure your dog gets the proper medication at the proper times, keep a calendar with the dates and times to administer the medication or put the times on your own personal day planner.

- Place the pill into a moist doggie treat or in some peanut butter. Your dog will never know it's there.

- Insert the pill into a piece of hot dog and give it to Rover.

Urine Samples

Your veterinarian may ask you to provide a sample of your dog's urine to analyze the sugar, blood, crystals, or other components. You may have to perform feats of acrobatics in order to catch a few drops as gravity pulls them from your dog onto the ground. If obtaining a urine sample has you mystified, try this:

- When you walk your dog, hold a paper cup or plastic container with a pair of long-handled tongs under your dog when he starts to urinate. Pour the urine into a clean glass jar and cap it. Needless to say, don't reuse the tongs at your family's next picnic!

When It's Time to Say Good-bye

Let's face it—pets are often our best friends. They are there during the most quiet, peaceful parts of our day. Pets love us even when others may not, and pets comfort and console us when we need it most. Because pets are such an important part of our lives, they leave an empty space when they pass away. If your dog has died, dealing with the grief that results is often difficult. Many people do not understand the depth to which a person may feel the loss of a pet as they do when we have lost a human loved one. In some circumstances, we may be left to deal with the loss without human support and consolation. If you would like to talk to someone who understands how you feel when your dog dies, see Resources at the end of this chapter for the telephone numbers of pet loss support hotlines. Although nothing can replace a beloved animal, there are ways in which we can help keep the memories alive and be comforted by them. Try one of these ideas to memorialize your lost dog.

• Keep a journal that describes the things that your dog did as a way of remembering the good times you had.

• Create a photo album or photo montage of your dog.

• Have a local artist paint a portrait of your dog.

• If you are handy with crafts, needlepoint a picture of your dog with his birth and death dates.

• Place a stone with your dog's name in your garden.

• Hold a memorial service for your dog that includes family and friends.

• Plant a tree, bush, or flower in remembrance of your dog.

• Make a donation to your favorite animal charity in your dog's name. Inquire if they have special donation categories such as putting a dog's name on a shelter cage or on a brick that becomes part of a new building.

- Gather up your dog's belongings and store them in a special container that you can retrieve when the pain heals.

- Place your dog's ashes in an urn to keep near.

- If you prefer to bury your pet in a cemetery, check local ones for those that have special pet burial locations. Or contact your local humane organization or shelter to see if they provide pet burial services. Put a memorial stone on his grave.

- If you have Internet access, visit The Pet Loss Grief Support web site and Candle Ceremony at *http://Petloss.com/* where you can list your dog's name.

- Contact your local humane society to see if they have a support group in which people meet to share their experiences. Often, it helps us deal with the loss of a pet to talk about it with other pet people who understand what we are going through.

Resources

Check out some of these books to help you care for your elderly or ill pet:

Gorman, Carl. *The Aging Dog: Helping Your Dog Through the Golden Years.* Ringpress Books Ltd., 1997.

Kejcz, Yvonne. *Guide to Owning an Aging Dog.* TFH Publications, 1997.

Simon, John, DVM, and Steve Duno. *Anti-Aging for Dogs.* St. Martin's Press, 1998.

Streitferdt, Uwe. *Healthy Dog, Happy Dog: A Complete Guide to Dog Diseases and Their Treatment.* Barron's Educational Series, Inc., 1994.

Pinney, Christopher. *Caring for Your Older Dog.* Barron's Educational Series, Inc., 1995.

For help dealing with grief over the loss of your pet, contact one of these pet loss support lines. Some support lines are staffed by veterinary students. Most lines operate only during specified times, but give you the option of leaving a message. Be aware that you will bear the costs for long-distance telephone calls. Return calls will be collect.

- Companion Animal Association of Arizona, 602-995-5885.

- Cornell University College of Veterinary Medicine, 607-253-3922.

- Ohio State University School of Veterinary Medicine, 614-292-1823.

- Tufts University School of Veterinary Medicine, 508-839-7966.

- University of California at Davis, 530-752-4200.

- University of Florida at Gainesville, 352-392-4700, ext. 4080.

- Virginia-Maryland Regional College of Veterinary Medicine, 540-231-8038.

Visit The Pet Loss Grief Support web site and Candle Ceremony at *http://Petloss.com/*.

Or visit the library or a bookstore for this book on dealing with pet loss:

Sife, Wallace. *The Loss of a Pet: New, Revised and Expanded Edition.* Howell Book House, 1998.

Helpful Hints for Dog Owners with Disabilities

Everyone who has ever owned a dog knows how beneficial one can be. Dogs provide us with love and companionship; they make us feel more relaxed and better equipped to handle the demands of daily life. Living with animals has been shown to lower blood pressure and reduce stress, even for those of us blessed with good health and no disabilities. But dogs are especially important to people with physical limitations or disabilities. Caring for a dog may mean the difference between feeling isolated and feeling as though a friend is always close at hand. Having an animal around that has been trained to assist those who suffer from physical limitations, blindness, or loss of hearing may mean the difference between functioning independently day to day or relying solely on the efforts of others. The other side of the coin, however, is that dogs need care. Those of us who may benefit the most from having a companion or service dog are often less able to care for one. The following tips are designed to help people who suffer from any one of a variety of different physical constraints, from arthritis and back conditions to wheelchair-bound difficulties and vision-related problems. Almost all of the tips came from other dog owners who have experienced the limitation in question.

Arthritis or Carpal Tunnel Syndrome

If you suffer from arthritis or any problems involving your hands, such as carpal tunnel syndrome, just opening a can of dog food can be a major ordeal. If you prepare your dog's food yourself, cutting and cooking it may not be much better in terms of the effort it takes and the stress it puts on your finger joints. The solution may be as simple as having the right tool for the right job. Check your local kitchen store for adaptive devices or see Resources at the end of this chapter for some on-line catalogs.

• Many dog foods come in flip-top cans. Some can be difficult to pull open. To help get the lid off, use a device that resembles a mini-bottle opener that slides under the tab to provide extra leverage. Or, try a product called Tab Eeze to safely open ring-top cans. If you cannot find such a device, simply open the can with a can opener as you would a can without a flip-top or flip it open with a bottle opener by inserting it under the tab.

• Electric can openers are easier to manipulate than hand can openers if your dog's food does not come in flip-top cans.

• If you must raise your dog's can of food until you reach a level of comfort for opening it, place one can on top of another. This is especially useful if you are feeding your pet the 5.5-ounce or similar size.

• Some of the tools available at kitchen or houseware stores have larger handles to make gripping easier.

• Kitchen tools with swivel handles assist you if your wrist rotation ability is limited so that you don't spill things off the spoon.

- If you have no strength in your hands, there is adaptive silver-ware that can attach to your hands for scooping out your dog's dinner.

- A V-shaped jar opener that attaches to the underside of a cup-board enables you to slide a jar into it, then turn the jar until the lid opens. This is useful for any dog product that comes in a jar with a lid or even for opening baby food if you must feed it to your dog if he is ill.

- As an alternative, use a round rubber device that you place on top of the jar lid to help you open it.

- To help you open boxes of your dog's dry food, use a device with a built-up handle that you simply insert and lift.

- For grooming your dog, attach to his brush a universal cuff or wrist cuff designed for people with limited hand strength to hold utensils. Slip your hand into the cuff and pull the brush over your dog.

- If you have trouble clipping your dog's leash onto his collar when you take him for a walk, use a choke collar and keep the leash attached to the collar rather than taking it on and off. When you bring your dog inside, simply slip the collar off with the leash attached.

Back Problems

As we age, flexibility may diminish and bending over becomes more difficult. Back surgery, degenerative spinal conditions, or even muscle spasms or temporary pain due to a variety of causes can prevent us from stooping over to pick up even the tiniest speck let alone a 50-pound bag of Fido's favorite food. Try some of these time-tested tips to help with tasks you need to perform when your back puts a *cramp* in your style.

- Large containers of dry food and cases of dog food are a way to save money, but those containers can be difficult to lift, especially if you have a back problem or experience weakness of some type. To transport heavy containers, use a child's wagon or a garbage can on wheels.

- Another solution to hauling those heavy pet food containers is to use a wheeled luggage cart. They are strong enough to carry at least 50-pound bags of food, inexpensive, and fold to a size that is easily slipped into the trunk of your car. Wheeled luggage carts are available in the luggage sections of department stores and can be found for about $10.

- Ask your local grocery store if they offer delivery service or check the Yellow Pages of your telephone directory for commercial delivery services that would pick up your dog's food for you.

- Purchase a long-handled scoop to minimize bending when getting dry food out of a large bag and placing it in your dog's dish. Some long-handled scoops double as pet food bag clasps to keep the bag closed and prevent excess air from making your dog's food stale.

- To take your dog to the veterinarian, use a wheeled pet carrier or a crate dolly.

- To groom your small dog, sit the dog on a table or countertop instead of getting down on the floor to groom. You will be able to brush and comb your dog without worrying how to get back up once you are down!

- To pick up doggie wastes from your yard, use a long-handled pet scoop or rake. They come in a variety of styles with handles up to 36 inches (91 cm) long.

- Getting your dog into a carrier then lifting him up at the groomer or veterinarian's office may be difficult. As an alternative, try carrying him in a backpack or sling tote specially designed for carrying pets under 15 pounds (7 kg).

• To lift and lower your dog's food and water bowls, use a long-handled dustpan.

• To eliminate the need to refill your dog's water dish as often, try one of the bowls in which you insert an upside-down 2-liter soda bottle that you fill with water. The water drains into a bowl for your dog to drink.

• If you have problems bending over to place food dishes on the floor, try feeding your dog on a bench or use an elevated food dish that comes in several heights. Elevated bowls hold both food and water and, in addition to making feeding your dog easier for you, they help aid his digestion and prevent intestinal disorders.

• Wall-mounted dog food and water bowls prevent bending over to refill them. To hang your dog's bowls from the wall at a height that is comfortable for you and your dog, purchase metal bowls and holders made to attach to wire dog kennel runs. Mount a metal towel rack available in discount department stores to the wall at the appropriate height. Hang the dog food bowl holder from the towel rack.

• Place your dog's dry food bag on a chair near the food stand or rack for easy dispensing.

HIV/AIDS

If you are a pet owner with HIV/AIDS, just walking your dog may require more effort than you can muster. Also, people who suffer from HIV/AIDS have a suppressed immune system that makes them susceptible to secondary infections and illnesses. Zoonotic diseases—those that can be transmitted from animals to people—are fairly uncommon and, in most cases, not life-threatening, but for the person with a suppressed immune system, zoonotic diseases may pose a special threat. If you are an HIV-positive dog owner, your pet poses a minimal risk to your health.

Parasites your dog could transmit include roundworms, hookworms, whipworms, cryptosporidia, and Giardia.

Having to give up a beloved canine companion during a time when you need him most but are least able to care for him adds a dimension of suffering that could be prevented. Before you find another home for your dog, try some of these suggestions to help you provide continuing care.

• As part of your dog's annual checkup, have his stools checked by a veterinarian for parasites and medicate your dog appropriately.

• Don't feed your dog raw or undercooked meats or unpasteurized milk.

• Practice good hygiene by keeping your surroundings clean. Use household bleach as a good germ killer or purchase an antibacterial cleaning product to eliminate germs from the place where your dog sleeps.

• Wear rubber gloves when cleaning up a doggie mess. Avoid direct contact with your dog's bodily fluids such as vomit, feces, urine, or saliva. Wash your hands and the gloves after cleaning up.

• If you've been bitten, rinse the wound or scratch right away with a mild soap and water.

• Contact a local chapter of Pets Are Wonderful Support (PAWS) or Pets Are Loving Support (PALS) to request a volunteer to help you with caring for your pet. PAWS groups operate nationwide and are dedicated to keeping pets with their HIV/AIDS owners. They can supply volunteers to lend a hand as well as information on keeping pets for the person who has been diagnosed with HIV. PAWS volunteers will clean, walk your dog, feed and water him, and provide other pet-related services. If no volunteers are available where you live, consider contacting a commercial service to help you care for your dog. Pet-sitters often offer additional services at a fee to pet owners who are incapacitated, so check the Yellow Pages under Pet-sitters.

• If you have no local PAWS chapter, contact your local AIDS resource center for advice on caring for your dog.

Vision Limitations

Losing one's sight either permanently or temporarily or even having it decreased due to cataracts or other causes can cause you to rethink how to manage everyday care of your dog. A dog, especially if he is a guide dog for the blind, will be your constant companion, but providing care for him may take some extra effort. Following are some tips for people with vision problems from people who have vision problems themselves. Some of the tips will help you if you've completely lost your vision, but others require that you have a minimum amount of vision and can discern shapes or contrasts.

• To help know where your dog is, put bells on his collar so that you can hear him when he walks around your home. If you have more than one dog, use different-sounding bells.

• To help you locate your dog, put his rabies tag and metal license next to each other on his collar so they jingle when he walks.

• Those of you that have vision problems know that your other senses learn to pick up the slack under such circumstances, so telling your dogs apart if you have more than one may be as simple as touching them and feeling their coats or sizes. If your dogs are the same size or their hair has a similar or identical feel, the process may be more difficult. To help differentiate the two dogs, put different types of collars on them. Use different combinations, such as a collar with a metal buckle and one with a plastic buckle or one collar made from elastic and the other one made from plastic to help you tell them apart.

• If you have a neighbor, relative, or friend who takes you grocery shopping or does it for you, peel the label from the food your dog likes and give it to the shopper so that he or she buys the correct variety or brand.

• Feeding your dogs a variety of flavors helps maintain their interest in their food. Put a rubber band around the cans of one flavor and not the other to be able to tell by feeling the presence of rubber bands which one you are feeding him. If you need more than two options, put two or three rubber bands on the different flavors.

• To measure quantities of food for your dog, keep the appropriate-sized measuring cup in the bag of food so you always will feed the correct amount.

• Place a tray with half-inch sides, such as a cookie sheet or pizza tray, along a wall where you are less likely to accidentally step on it. When you feed your dog, place his food and water on the tray. Anything that spills from his bowl will fall onto the tray. To clean it, simply lift the entire tray and dump the fallen bits into the garbage disposal or trash can.

• If you have no one who can take you and your dog to the veterinarian, find out if there is someone in your vicinity who provides taxi service for your veterinary trips. A pet-sitter or pet care professional also may have such a service. Check the Yellow Pages of your phone directory under Pets or Pet-sitters. Inquire at local pet stores if none are listed in the telephone directory.

• Some veterinarians make house calls, so, if transportation is a problem for you, find a veterinarian who will come to your home.

• If you must give your dog medication, ask for it in pill form so that you don't have to measure dosages in a dropper. Place one hand over your dog's head and open his mouth with your thumb and forefinger. Pop the pill in his mouth with your other hand.

• If the medicine comes in a capsule and must be divided, open the capsule and pour the white powder onto a dark tile or board, for contrast, that you've placed on your kitchen counter. Divide the powder into parts with a razor blade. Sprinkle the portion over your dog's food and mix it in.

• To tell if your dog is sick, pay attention to his activity level and touch his nose. A dry nose along with diminished activity may indicate that your dog isn't feeling well.

• If blindness or vision problems prevent you from functioning, investigate obtaining a guide dog. A guide dog may be your link to the world and help you live a full and normal life. See Resources at the end of this chapter for more information.

• To clean up your dog's wastes, keep him on leash. If your dog stops, run your hand down his back. If his back is curved and he is hunched over, you know that he is moving his bowels. Stand still and, based on where your dog is standing, follow along his back toward the tail to determine where the deposit is. Insert your hand in a plastic bag, pick up the wastes, and pull them inside the bag. Tie the bag and throw it in the trash.

• To keep your dog from causing you to trip, teach him to go to a special place when he is not with you. Show your dog the place and give a command. Keep the command consistent and repeat the process until your dog knows to go to his special place when you say the command. Praise your dog each time he follows directions. Put one or two of your dog's special chew toys in the place to make the spot more appealing.

Weakness

In some cases, degenerative conditions may cause us to become weak and unable to perform tasks that require a certain amount of strength. If caring for your dog has become difficult because of weakness, here are some suggestions for strengthening your physical resources.

- When it comes time for your dog to visit the veterinarian, investigate mobile veterinarians who will come to your house to see your pet. Mobile veterinarians are especially helpful if you have large dogs or several pets. The mobile veterinarian can check on all of the pets at one time and give each one his annual vaccinations in one visit. Check the Yellow Pages of your telephone directory under Veterinarians for listings.

- If you must have your dog groomed, contact a groomer who operates a mobile facility and, like mobile veterinarians, will come to your home to conduct the necessary grooming.

- If you need help giving your dog medicine, fluids, or shots, ask your veterinarian if he or she knows of anyone who will make home visits. If not, contact local pet-sitters to find ones who will assist you. Many pet-sitters are trained to perform these functions for the sick pet for owners who cannot perform them for themselves or for owners when they are away.

- When feeding and watering your dog, use large bowls so that you don't have to refill them as often.

- Ask a friend or neighbor to divide your dog's food into smaller containers so that you can lift what you need more easily.

- To play with your dog, use flashlights or laser pointers. Dogs love chasing the light, and you won't have to make a move.

- If you have difficulty performing basic functions for yourself, investigate the use of a service or assistance dog. Assistance dogs are trained to help people with physical limitations perform their everyday functions. Assistance dogs are accepted in public places just as guide dogs and hearing dogs are. See Resources at the end of this chapter for locations that provide assistance dogs.

- If you are planning to get a dog, find one with an activity level that is less than yours. Dogs do a great job forcing their owners to get exercise and fresh air each day, but an overly active dog can be a handful when your energy hits bottom. Before adopting or purchasing a dog, investigate the breed characteristics and think twice about bringing home one of the more active breeds.

• A dog, even a small one, may be able to pull the leash out of your hand or even pull you to the ground if you suffer from weakness. Walking your dog in ice or snow may be completely out of the question. As an alternative, use a radio collar as a virtual leash when your dog needs to go outside to potty. In time and with practice, you may not have to activate the radio collar because your dog will know the spatial boundaries you have set.

Wheelchair-Bound

Being confined to a wheelchair poses a whole set of problems when it comes to caring for ourselves and our pets. Because a person in a wheelchair is constantly seated, everything that is either above or below arm's length is simply out of reach. Try some of these suggestions for getting a grip on caring for your dog.

• Use a long-handled device that looks like a tong and has a "jaw" on one end, designed to help people reach and grab items out of their grasp. Useful when grocery shopping, the arm-extending device is also useful at home to grab your dog's food from the cupboard or counter top.

• Extend your reach with long-handled kitchen tools, commonly used for barbecuing, that are also useful for lifting pet bowls to and from the floor. Tongs and sturdy spatulas allow you to pick up and lower your dog's food and water dishes.

• As an alternative, use a long-handled dustpan to raise and lower your dog's food dishes to the floor.

- To have water available for your dog when you need it, have someone fill plastic gallon jugs with water and put them on the floor near his water dish. This makes it easy to fill the bowls when seated.

- Put your dog's canned food in a "soda chute" designed to hold cans of soda in the refrigerator. Placed in the cupboard, the soda chute will dispense cans of dog food and keep you from having to reach to the back of the cupboard for them.

- If getting to the veterinarian is difficult, find a mobile veterinary clinic that will come to your home.

- If you are able to drive, but getting your dog and your wheelchair into your veterinarian's office is cumbersome, ask if anyone can meet you at the car to help.

- Purchase a raised stand to hold both food and water bowls to avoid having to pick them up off the floor.

- A long-handled pet scoop helps you reach your dog's droppings from a wheelchair. Place the wastes in a plastic bag for easy disposal.

- To take your dog for a stroll, use a retractable, nylon leash so that your dog can walk up to 26 feet (8 m) looking for just the right spot to potty while you stay put. Flexible leashes come in a variety of lengths for dogs of all sizes, even service dogs. Complete control is obtained by using only one hand to operate the retractable leash.

- Keep a 50-foot (15-m) tie-out in the backyard so that your dog will have ample room to run around and the lead will reach to your back door when it's time for your dog to come in or be let out.

- Determine if there is a neighborhood child who likes to earn extra money by giving dogs a bath when it comes time to wash the dirt off your pooch.

Resources

These books describe the work of the assistance dog:

Eames, Ed, and Mordecai Siegal. *Partners in Independence: A Success Story of Dogs and the Disabled.* Howell Book House, 1997.

Putnam, Peter. *Love in the Lead: The Miracle of the Seeing Eye Dog.* University Press of America, September 1998.

For more information about obtaining a service dog, contact one of these organizations:

International Association of Assistance Dog Partners (IAADP): IAADP is a nonprofit, cross-disability organization launched in 1993 representing people partnered with guide, hearing, and service dogs. IAADP's stated mission is to provide assistance dog partners with a voice in the assistance dog field; enable those partnered with guide dogs, hearing dogs, and service dogs to work together on issues of mutual concern; and foster the disabled person/assistance dog partnership. IAADP can be reached at

P.O. Box 1326
Sterling Heights, MI 48311
Tel: 810-826-3938.
ismi.net/iaadp

Guide Dogs for the Blind, Inc.
P.O. Box 151200
San Rafael, CA 94915-1200
Tel: 415-499-4000 or 800-295-4050
guidedogs.com/

If you suffer from HIV/AIDS, visit the San Francisco PAWS web page for a listing of chapters nationwide at *pawssf.org/chapters.html.*

Following are two vendors of assistance devices for the elderly and disabled.

🐾 Assistive Devices, Inc., in Austin, TX, 800-856-0889 or *http://www.geocel.com/adi/*

🐾 CARE4U—Aids for Daily Living only on the Web at *care4u.com/*

For additional adaptive kitchen devices, visit a kitchen supply store.

On-line and Print Pet Supply Sources

Internet Pet Stores

Pet supply stores on the Internet will deliver food, toys, and other supplies to your door.

Amazon.com for dog books
Pet Planet: *www.petplanet.com*
Petopia: *www.petopia.com*
The Pet Channel: *www.thepetchannel.com*
The Pet Store: *www.petstore.com*

Pet Supply Catalogs

If you would like to mail-order pet products, try perusing these pet supply catalogs.

Cherrybrook
Route 57, Box 15
Broadway, NJ 08808
908-689-7979 (inside NJ)
1-800-524-0820

The Humane Catalog
The Humane Society of the United States
P.O. Box 1519
Elmira, NY 14902-1723
hsus.org

J-B Wholesale Pet Supplies
289 Wagaraw Road
Hawthorne, NJ 07506

New England Serum Company
P.O. Box 128
Topsfield, MA 01983-0228
1-800-637-3786

PetExpo
11525 Manchaca Rd., Suite 101
Austin, TX 78748
512-292-4738
www.pet-expo.com

South PAW
8 Colleen Circle
Ewing, NJ 08638
1-888-251-8689
www.southpawpets.com

That Pet Place
237 Centerville Road
Lancaster, PA 17603
1-800-THAT PET
www.thatpetplace.com

Valley Vet Supply
1-800-531-2390
www.valleyvet.com

Index

BARRON'S BOOKS FOR DOG OWNERS

Barron's offers a wonderful variety of books for dog owners and prospective owners, all written by experienced breeders, trainers, veterinarians, or qualified experts on canines. Most books are heavily illustrated with handsome color photos and instructive line art. They'll tell you facts you need to know, and give you advice on purchasing, feeding, grooming, training, and keeping a healthy pet.

Before You Buy That Puppy
ISBN 0-8120-1750-1

Careers with Dogs
ISBN 0-7641-0503-5

Caring for Your Older Dog
ISBN 0-8120-9149-3

Civilizing Your Puppy, 2nd Ed.
ISBN 0-8120-9787-4

Communicating with Your Dog
ISBN 0-7641-0758-5

Compatible Canines
ISBN 0-7641-0724-0

**The Complete Book of
Dog Breeding**
ISBN 0-8120-9604-5

The Complete Book of Dog Care
ISBN 0-8120-4158-5

The Complete Guide to the Dog
ISBN 0-7641-5204-1

The Dog: A Child's Friend
ISBN 0-7641-0302-4

**The Dog Owner's Question
and Answer Book**
ISBN 0-7641-0647-3

Educating Your Dog
ISBN 0-8120-9592-8

Encyclopedia of Dog Breeds
ISBN 0-7641-5097-9

Fun and Games with Your Dog
ISBN 0-8120-9721-1

**Healthy Dog, Happy Dog:
A Complete Guide to Dog
Diseases and Their Treatments**
ISBN 0-8120-1842-7

**How to Teach Your
Old Dog New Tricks**
ISBN 0-8120-4544-0

**Natural Health Care
for Your Dog**
ISBN 0-7641-0122-6

The Dog Handbook
ISBN 0-7641-1152-3

The New Terrier Handbook
ISBN 0-8120-3951-3

**101 Questions Your
Dog Would Ask**
ISBN 0-7641-0886-7

Puppies
ISBN 0-7641-1601-0

**Saved! A Guide to Success
with Your Shelter Dog**
ISBN 0-7641-0062-9

Show Me!
ISBN 0-8120-9710-6

Train Your Dog
ISBN 0-7641-0967-7

The Trick Is in the Training
ISBN 0-7641-0492-6

The Well-Behaved Dog
ISBN 0-7641-5066-9

Barron's Educational Series, Inc.
250 Wireless Blvd., Hauppauge, NY 11788 • To order toll-free: 1-800-645-3476
In Canada: Georgetown Book Warehouse • 34 Armstrong Ave., Georgetown, Ont. L7G 4R9
Order toll free in Canada: 1-800-247-7160
Or order from your favorite bookstore or pet store
Visit our web site at: www.barronseduc.com

(#111) 12/00